Henry Drummond.

TROPICAL AFRICA

BY

HENRY DRUMMOND, LL.D., F.R.S.E.

AUTHOR OF " NATURAL LAW IN THE SPIRITUAL WORLD."

NEGRO UNIVERSITIES PRESS
NEW YORK

DT
361
D8
1969

Originally published in 1890
by John B. Alden, Publisher, New York

Reprinted 1969 by
Negro Universities Press
A DIVISION OF GREENWOOD PUBLISHING CORP.
NEW YORK

SBN 8371-2266-X

PRINTED IN UNITED STATES OF AMERICA

CONTENTS.

PREFACE.

It is the genial tax of literature upon Travel that those who have explored the regions of the uncivilised should open their bag of wonders before the world and celebrate their return to clothing in three or four volumes and a map. This exaction, in the nature of things, must shortly abolish itself.

As a minor traveller, whose assets are few, I have struggled to evade even this obligation, but having recently had to lecture on African subjects to various learned and unlearned Societies in England and America, it has been urged upon me that a few of the lecture-notes thrown into popular form might be useful as a general sketch of East Central Africa. Great books of travel have had their day. But small books, with the larger features of a country lightly sketched, and just enough of narrative to make you feel that you are really there, have a function in helping the imagination of those who have not breath enough to keep up with the great explorers.

The publication of " The White Ant " and " Mimicry " has been already forestalled by one of the monthly magazines; and the " Geological Sketch " is rescued, and duly dusted, from the archives of the British Association. If the dust of science has been too freely shaken from the other chapters, the scientific reader will overlook it for the sake of an overworked public which has infinite trouble in getting itself mildly instructed and entertained without being disheartened by the heavy pomp of technical expression.

If anything in a work of this class could pretend to a serious purpose, I do not conceal that, in addition to the mere desire to inform, a special reason exists just now for writing about Africa—a reason so urgent that I excuse myself with difficulty for introducing so grave a problem in so slight a setting. The reader who runs his eye over the " Heart-Disease of Africa" will discover how great the need is for arousing afresh that truer interest in the Dark Centinent which since Livingstone's time has almost died away. To many modern travellers Africa is simply a country to be explored ; to Livingstone it was a land to be pitied and redeemed. And recent events on Lake Nyassa have stirred a new desire in the hearts of those who care for native Africa that " the open sore of the world" should have a last and decisive treatment at the hands of England.

HENRY DRUMMOND.

TROPICAL AFRICA.

I

THE WATER-ROUTE TO THE HEART OF AFRICA.

THE ZAMBESI AND SHIRE.

THREE distinct Africas are known to the modern world—North Africa, where men go for health; South Africa, where they go for money; and Central Africa, where they go for adventure. The first, the old Africa of Augustine and Carthage, every one knows from history; the geography of the second, the Africa of the Zulu and the diamond, has been taught us by two Universal Educators—War and the Stock-Exchange; but our knowledge of the third, the Africa of Livingstone and Stanley, is still fitly symbolized by the vacant look upon our maps which tells how long this mysterious land has kept its secret.

Into the heart of this mysterious Africa I wish to take you with me now. And let me mangify my subject by saying at once that it is a wonderful thing to see. It is a wonderful thing to start from the civilization of Europe, pass up these mighty rivers, and work your way into that unknown land—work your way alone, and on foot, mile after mile, month after month, among strange birds and beasts and plants and insects, meeting tribes which have no name, speaking tongues which no man can interpret, till you have reached its secret heart, and stood where white man has never trod before. It is a wonderful thing to look at this weird world of human beings—half animal half children, wholly savage and wholly heathen ; and to turn and come back again to civilization before the impressions have had time to fade, and while the myriad problems of so strange' a spectacle are still seething in the mind. It is an education to see this sight—an education in the meaning and history of man. To have been here is to have lived before Menes. It is to have watched the dawn of evolution. It is to have the great moral and social problems of life, of anthropology, of ethnology, and even of theology, brought home to the imagination in the most new and startling light.

On the longest day of a recent summer—midwinter therefore in the tropics—I left London. A long railway run across France, Switzerland, and Italy brings one in a day or two to the Mediterranean. Crossing to Alexandria, the traveller strikes across Egypt over the Nile, through the battlefield of Tel-el-Kebir, to the Red Sea, steams down its sweltering length to Aden, tranships, and, after three lifetimes of deplorable humiliation in the south-west Monsoons, terminates his sufferings at Zanzibar.

Zanzibar is the focus of all East African exploration. No matter where you are going in the interior, you must begin at Zanzibar. Oriental in its appearance, Mohammedan in its religion, Arabian in its morals, this cesspool of wickedness is a fit capital for the Dark Continent. But Zanzibar is Zanzibar simply because it is the only apology for a town on the whole coast. An immense outfit is required to penetrate this shopless and foodless land, and here only can the traveller make up his caravan. The ivory and slave trades have made caravaning a profession, and everything the explorer wants is to be had in these bazaars, from a tin of sardines to a repeating rifle. Here these black villains, the porters, the necessity and the despair of travellers, the scum of old slave gangs, and the fugitives from justice from every tribe, congregate for hire. And if there is one thing on which African travellers are for once agreed, it is that for laziness, ugliness, stupidness, and wickedness, these men are not to be matched on any continent in the world. Their one strong point is that they will engage themselves for the Victoria Nyanza or for the Grand Tour of the Tanganyika with as little ado as a Chamounix guide volunteers for the Jardin; but this singular avidity is mainly due to the fact that each man cherishes the hope of running away at the earliest opportunity. Were it only to avoid requiring to employ these gentlemen, having them for one's sole company month after month, seeing them transgress every commandment in turn before your eyes—you yourself being powerless to check them except by a wholesale breach of the sixth—it would be worth while to seek another route into the heart of Africa.

But there is a much graver objection to the Zanzibar route to the interior. Stanley started by this route on his search for Livingstone, two white men with him; he came back without them. Cameron set out by the same path to cross Africa with two companions; before he got to Tanganyika he was alone. The Geographical Society's late expedition, under Mr. Keith Johnstone, started from Zanzibar with two Europeans; the hardy and accomplished leader fell within a couple of months. These expeditions have all gone into the interior by this one fatal way, and probably every second man, by fever or by accident, has left his bones to bleach along the road. Hitherto there has been no help for it. The great malarious coast-belt must be crossed, and one had simply to take his life in his hands and go through with it.

But now there is an alternative. There is a rival route into the interior, which, though it is not without its dark places too, will probably yet become the

great highway from the East to Central Africa.
Let me briefly sketch it:

Africa, speaking generally, is a vast, ill-formed
triangle. It has no peninsulas; it has almost no
islands or bays or fjords. But three great inlets, three
mighty rivers piercing it to the very heart, have been
allocated by a kind Nature, one to each of its solid
sides. On the north is the river of the past, flow-
ing through Egypt, as Leigh Hunt says, " like some
grave, mighty thought threading a dream"; on the
west, the river of the future, the not less mysterious
Congo; and on the east the little known Zambesi.

The physical features of this great continent are
easily grasped. From the coast a low scorched plain,
reeking with malaria, extends inland in unbroken
monotony for two or three hundred miles. This is
succeeded by mountains slowly rising into a plateau
some 2000 or 3000 feet high; and this, at some hundreds of miles distance, forms the pedestal for a second
plateau, as high again. This last plateau, 4000 to
5000 feet high, may be said to occupy the whole of
Central Africa. It is only on the large scale, however, that these are to be reckoned plateaux at all.
When one is upon them he sees nothing but mountains and valleys and plains of the ordinary type,
covered for the most part with forest.

I have said that Nature has supplied each side of
Africa with one great river. By going some hundreds
of miles southward along the coast from Zanzibar the
traveller reaches the mouth of the Zambesi. Livingstone sailed up this river once, and about a hundred miles from its mouth discovered another river
twisting away northwards among the mountains.
The great explorer was not the man to lose such a
chance of penetrating the interior. He followed this
river up, and after many wanderings found himself
on the shores of a mighty lake. The river is named
the Shiré, and the lake—the existence of which was
quite unknown before, is Lake Nyassa. Lake Nyassa

is 350 miles long; so that, with the Zambesi, the Shiré, and this great lake, we have the one thing required to open up East Central Africa—a water-route to the interior. But this is not all. Two hundred and fifty miles from the end of Lake Nyassa another lake of still nobler proportions takes up the thread of communication. Lake Tanganyika is 450 miles in length. Between the lakes stands a lofty plateau, cool, healthy. accessible, and without any physical barrier to interrupt the explorer's march. By this route the Victoria Nyanza and the Albert Nyanza may be approached with less fatigue, less risk, and not less speed, than by the overland trail from Zanzibar. At one point also, along this line, one is within a short march of that other great route which must ever be regarded as the trunk-line of the African continent. The watershed of the *Congo* lies on this Nyassa-Tanganyika plateau. This is the stupendous natural highway on which so much of the future of East Central Africa must yet depend.

Ten days' languid steaming from Zanzibar brings the traveller to the Zambesi mouth. The bar here has an evil reputation, and the port is fixed on a little river which flows into the Indian Ocean slightly to the north, but the upper reaches of which almost join the Zambesi at some distance inland. This port is the Portuguese settlement of Quilimane, and here I said good-bye to the steamer and to civilization. Some distance in the interior stands a solitary pioneer Mission station of the Established Church of Scotland, and still farther in, on Lake Nyassa, another outpost of a sister church. My route led past both these stations, and I had the good fortune to pick up on the way two or three young fellow-countrymen who were going up to relieve the mission staff. For the latter part of my journey I was quite alone. All African work, as a rule, is done single-handed. It is not always easy to find a companion for such a project, and the climate is so pestilential that when two go, you and your friend are simply nursing each other time about, and the expedition never gets on. On the whole, however, the solitary course is not to be commended. An unutterable loneliness comes over one at times in the great still forests, and there is a stage in African fever—and every one *must* have fever—when the watchful hand of a friend may make the difference between life and death.

After leaving Quilimane, the first week of our journey up the Qua-qua was one long picnic. We had two small row-boats, the sterns covered with a sun-proof awning, and under these we basked, and talked, and read and prospected, from dawn to sunset. Each boat was paddled by seven or eight natives—muscular heathens, whose sole dress was a pocket-handkerchief, a little palm oil, and a few mosquitoes. Except at first the river was only a few yards broad, and changed in character and novelty every hour. Now it ran through a grove of cocoa-nut palms—the most wonderful and beautiful tree of the tropics. Now its sullen current oozed through a fœtid swamp of mangroves—the home of the crocodile and the hippopotamus, whose slimy bodies wallowed into the pools with a splash as our boats sped past. Again the banks became green and graceful, the long plumed grasses bending to the stream, and the whole a living aviary of birds —the white ibis and the gaunt fish eagle, and the exquisite blue and scarlet kingfisher watching its prey from the overhanging boughs. The business-like air of this last bird is almost comical, and somehow sits ill on a creature of such gorgeous beauty. One expects him to flutter away before the approach of so material a thing as a boat, display his fairy plumage in a few airy movements, and melt away in the sunshine. But there he sits, stolid and impassive, and though the spray of the paddles almost dashes in his face, the intent eyes never move, and he refuses to acknowledge the intruder by so much as a glance.

His larger ally, the black and white spotted king-fisher, if less beautiful, is much more energetic, and darts about the bank incessantly, coquetting with the boat from reach to reach, and seldom allowing an inspection close enough to take in the details of his piebald coat.

One interests oneself in these things more par-ticularly because there is nothing at first especially striking about the river scenery itself. Ten or twenty feet of bank cuts off the view on either side, and large and varied features are wanting. The banks are lined with the densest jungle of mangroves and aquatic grasses, while creepers of a hundred kinds struggle for life among the interlacing stems. We saw crocodiles here in such numbers that count was very soon lost. They were of all sizes, from the baby specimen which one might take home in a bottle to the enormous bullet-proof brute the size of an 81-ton gun. These revolting animals take their siesta in the heat of the day, lying prone upon the bank, with their wedge-shaped heads directed to-wards the water. When disturbed they scuttle into the river with a wriggling movement, the precipitancy of which defies the power of sight. The adjustment of the adult crocodile to its environment in the matter of color is quite remarkable. The younger forms are lighter yellow, and more easily discoverable, but it takes the careful use of a good pair of eyes to dis-tinguish in the gnarled slime-covered log lying among the rotting stumps the living form of the mature specimen. Between the African crocodiles and the alligators there is the slightest possible external dif-ference; although the longer head, the arrangement of scales, the fringed feet with their webbed toes, the uniform teeth, and the protrusion of the large canine, distinguish them from their American allies.

Many of the ibises I shot as we moved along, for food for the men, who, like all Africans, will do any-thing for flesh in whatever form. For ourselves, we lived upon emaciated fowls and tinned meats cooking them at a fire on the bank when the boat stopped. Eggs are never eaten by the natives, but always set; although, if you offer to buy them, the natives will bring you a dozen from a sitting hen, which they assure you were laid that very morning. In the interior, on many occasions afterwards, these protestations were tested, and always proved false. One time, when nearly famished and far from camp, I was brought a few eggs which a chief himself guaranteed had that very hour been laid. With sincere hope that he might be right, but with much misgiving, I ordered the two freshest looking to be boiled. With the despair of a starving man I opened them. They were cock and hen.

Breakfast and luncheon and dinner are all the same in Africa. There is no beef, nor mutton, nor bread, nor flour, nor sugar, nor salt, nor anything whatever, except an occasional fowl, which an Englishman can eat. Hence the enormous outfit which he must carry with him. No one has any idea of what can be had in tins till he camps out abroad. Every conceivable digestible and indigestible is to be had tinned, every form of fish, flesh, fowl, and game, every species of vegetable, and fruit, every soup, sweet, and *entrée*; but after two or three months of this sort of thing you learn that this tempting semblance of variety is a gigantic imposition. The sole difference between these various articles lies, like the Rhine wines, in the label. Plum pudding or kippered herring taste just the same. Whether you begin dinner with tinned calves-foot jelly or end with tinned salmon makes no difference; and after six months it is only by a slight feeling of hardness that you do not swallow the tins themselves.

At the end of a too short week we left our boats behind. Engaging an army of shy natives at a few huts near the bank, we struck across a low neck of land, and after an hour's walk found ourselves sud-

denly on the banks of the Zambesi. A solitary bun-
galow was in sight, and opposite it the little steamer
of the African Lakes Company, which was to take us
up the Shiré. There is more in the association,
perhaps, than in the landscape, to strike one as he
first furrows the waters of this virgin river. We are
fifty miles from its mouth, the mile-wide water
shallow and brown, the low sandy banks fringed with
alligators and wild birds. The great deltoid plain,
yellow with sun-tanned reeds and sparsely covered
with trees, stretches on every side; the sun is blister-
ing hot; the sky, as it will be for months, a monotonous dome of blue—not a frank bright blue like
the Canadian sky, but a veiled blue, a suspicious and
malarious blue, partly due to the perpetual heat haze
and partly to the imagination, for the Zambesi is no
friend to the European, and this whole region is
heavy with depressing memories.

This impression, perhaps, was heightened by the
fact that we were to spend that night within a few
yards of the place where Mrs. Livingstone died.
Late in the afternoon we reached the spot—a low
ruined hut a hundred yards from the river's bank,
with a broad verandah shading its crumbling walls.
A grass-grown path straggled to the doorway, and the
fresh print of a hippopotamus told how neglected the
spot is now. Pushing the door open, we found ourselves in a long dark room, its mud floor broken into
fragments, and remains of native fires betraying its
latest occupants. Turning to the right, we entered
a smaller chamber, the walls bare and stained, with
two glassless windows facing the river. The evening
sun setting over the far-off Morumballa mountains,
filled the room with its soft glow, and took our
thoughts back to that Sunday evening twenty years
ago, when in this same bedroom, at this same hour,
Livingstone knelt over his dying wife, and witnessed the great sunset of his life,

Under a huge baobab tree—a miracle of vegetable

vitality and luxuriance—stands Mrs. Livingstone's grave. The picture in Livingstone's book represents the place as well kept and surrounded with neatly-planted trees. But now it is an utter wilderness, matted with jungle grass and trodden by the beasts of the forest; and as I looked at the forsaken mound and contrasted it with her husband's tomb in Westminster Abbey, I thought perhaps the woman's love which brought her to a spot like this might be not less worthy of immortality.

The Zambesi is the great river of Eastern Africa, and, after the Congo, the Nile, and the Niger, the most important on the continent. Rising in the far interior among the marshes of Lake Dilolo, and, gathering volume from the streams which flow from the high lands connecting the north of Lake Nyassa with Inner Angola, it curves across the country for over a thousand miles like an attenuated letter S, and before its four great mouths empty the far-travelled waters into the Indian Ocean, drains an area of more than half a million square miles. As it cuts its way down the successive steps of the central plateaux its usually placid current is interrupted by rapids, narrows, cascades, and cataracts, corresponding to the plateau edges, so that like all the rivers of Africa it is only navigable in stretches of one or two hundred miles at a time. From the coast the Zambesi might be stemmed by steam-power to the rapids of Kebra-basa; and from above that point intermittently, as far as the impassable barrier of the Victoria Falls. Above this, for some distance, again follow rapids and water-falls, but these are at length succeeded by an unbroken chain of tributaries which together form an inland waterway of a thousand miles in length. The broad lands along the banks of this noble river are subject to annual inundations like the region of the Nile, and hence their agricultural possibilities are unlimited. On the lower Zambesi, indigo, the orchila weed, and calumba-root abound, and oil-seeds and sugar-cane could be produced in quantity to supply the whole of Europe. At present, owing to apathy and indifferent government, these magnificent resources are almost wholly undeveloped.

Next afternoon our little vessel left the Zambesi in its wake and struck up a fine lake-like expansion to the north, which represents the mouth of the Shiré. Narrower and deeper, the tributary is a better stream for navigation than the Zambesi. The scenery also is really fine, especially as one nears the mountains of the plateau, and the strange peoples and animals along the banks occupy the mind with perpetual interests. The hippopotami, prowling round the boat and tromboning at us within pistol-shot, kept us awake at night; and during the day we could see elephants, buffaloes, deer, and other large game wandering about the banks. To see the elephant at home is a sight to remember. The stupendous awkwardness of the menagerie animal, as if so large a creature were quite a mistake, vanishes completely when you watch him in his native haunts. Here he is as nimble as a kitten, and you see how perfectly this moving mountain is adapted to its habitat—how such a ponderous monster, indeed, is as natural to these colossal grasses as a rabbit to an English park. We were extremely fortunate in seeing elephants at all at this stage, and I question whether there is any other part of Africa where these animals may be observed leisurely and in safety within six weeks of London. Mr. Stanley in his Livingstone expedition was ten months in the country before he saw any; and Mr. Joseph Thomson, during his long journey to Tanganyika and back, never came across a single elephant. It is said that the whale which all travellers see in crossing the Atlantic is kept up by the steamboat companies, but I vouch that these Shiré valley elephants are independent of subsidy.

The question of the disappearance of the elephant here and throughout Africa is, as every one knows,

only one of a few years. It is hard to think why
this kindly and sagacious creature should have to be
exterminated; why this vast store of animal energy,
which might be turned into so much useful work,
should be lost to civilization. But the causes are
not difficult to understand. The African elephant
has never been successfully tamed, and is therefore
a failure as a source of energy. As a source of ivory,
on the other hand, he has been but too great a success.
The cost of ivory at present is about half-a-sovereign
per pound. An average tusk weighs from twenty
to thirty pounds. Each animal has two, and in Africa
both male and female carry tusks. The average
elephant is therefore worth in pounds sterling the
weight in pounds avoirdupois of one of his tusks. I
have frequently seen single tusks turning the scale
upon ninety pounds, the pair in this case being worth
nearly £100 sterling,—so that a herd of elephants is
about as valuable as a gold mine. The temptation to
sacrifice the animal for his tusks is therefore great;
and as he becomes scarcer he will be pursued by the
hunter with ever-increasing eagerness. But the truth
is, sad though the confession be, the sooner the last
elephant falls before the hunters bullet the better for
Africa. Ivory introduces into the country at present
an abnormal state of things. Upon this one article
is set so enormous a premium that none other among
African products secures the slightest general attention; nor will almost anyone in the interior con-
descend to touch the normal wealth, or develop the
legitimate industries of the country, so long as a tusk
remains. In addition to this, of half the real woes
which now exist in Africa ivory is at the bottom.
It is not only that wherever there is an article to
which a fictitious value is attached the effect upon
the producer is apt to be injurious; nor that wherever
there is money there is temptation, covetousness, and
war; but that unprincipled men, and especially Arabs,
are brought into contact with the natives in the worst

relation, influence them only in one, and that the lowest, direction, and leave them always worse than they find them—worse in greed, in knavery, in their belief in mankind, and in their suspicion of civilization. Further, for every tusk an Arab trader purchases he must buy, borrow, or steal a slave to carry it to the coast. Domestic slavery is bad enough, but now begins the long slave-march with its untold horrors—horrors instigated and perpetuated almost solely by the traffic in ivory. The extermination of the elephant, therefore, will mark one stage at least in the closing up of the slave-trade. The elephant has done much for Africa. The best he can do now for his country is to disappear forever.

In books of travel great chiefs are usually called kings, their wives queens, while their mud-huts are always palaces. But after seeing my first African chief at home, I found I must either change my views of kings or of authors. The regal splendor of Chipitula's court—and Chipitula was a very great chief indeed, and owned all the Shiré district—may be judged of by the fact that when I paid my respects to his highness his court-dress consisted almost exclusively of a pair of suspenders. I made this king happy for life by the gift of a scarlet tennis-cap and a few buttons. But poor Chipitula had not long to enjoy his treasures,—and I mention the incident to show what is going on every day in Africa. When I came back that way, on my return journey, I called again to receive a leopard skin which this chief had promised to trap for me, and for which he was to get in exchange certain dilapidated remnants of my wardrobe. He gave me the skin; I duly covered his, and we parted. A few days after, another white man came that way; he was a trader—the only one who has yet plied this hazardous calling in East Central Africa. He quarrelled with Chipitula over some bargain, and in a moment of passion drew his revolver and shot the chief dead on the spot. Of course

he himself was instantly speared by Chipitula's men ;
and all his black porters, according to native etiquette,
were butchered with their master.   There is absolutely no law in Africa, and you can kill anybody
and anybody can kill you, and no one will ask any
questions.

  Our next stoppage was to pay another homage—
truly this is a tragic region—at another white man's
grave. A few years ago Bishop Mackenzie and
some other missionaries were sent to Africa by the
English Universities, with instructions to try to
establish a Mission in the footsteps of Livingstone.
They came here ; the climate overpowered them ; one
by one they sickened and died.   With the death of
the Bishop himself the site was abandoned, and the
few survivors returned home.   Among the hippo-
potamus-trampled reeds on the banks of the Shiré
under a rough iron cross, lies the first of three brave
bishops who have already made their graves in
Equatorial Africa.

  I have spoken of the Shiré as the great waterway
into the interior of Eastern Africa.   It has one defect.
After sailing for five or six days we came to rapids
which no boat can pass.   These rapids were named
by Livingstone the Murchison Cataracts, and they
extend for seventy miles. This distance, accordingly,
must be traversed overland.   Half-way up this seventy miles, and a considerable distance inland from
the river, stands the first white settlement in East
Central Africa—the Blantyre Mission. Bribing about
a hundred natives with a promise of a fathom of calico
each, to carry our luggage, we set off on foot for
Blantyre.   The traditional characteristics of African
caravaning were displayed in full perfection during
this first experience, and darkness fell when we were
but half-way to our destination.   It was our first night
in the bush, and a somewhat unusual introduction to
African travelling marked it.   At midnight we were
roused by startling cries from our men, who lay sleep-

ing on the ground around us. The watch-fires must have burned down, for a lion had suddenly sprung into the camp. Seizing the man who lay nearest the forest, the animal buried its claws in his breast, and was making off into the darkness, when the shouting frightened it and made it drop its prey. Twice during the night the lion came back, and we whites had to keep watch by turns till morning with loaded rifles. This is altogether an exceptional case, for with a good fire one can generally spread his mat anywhere in the tropics without fear of midnight attack. This is a famous place, however, for lions, and one can as certainly depend on their gruesome concert in the early morning as on the sparrows' chirp in England.

Towards sunset the following evening our caravan filed into Blantyre. On the beauty and interest of this ideal mission I shall not dwell. But if anyone wishes to find out what can be done with the virgin African, what can be done by broad and practical missionary methods, let him visit the Rev. D. Clement Scott and his friends at Blantyre. And if he wishes to observe the possibilities of civilization and colonization among an average African tribe living on an average African soil, let him examine the mission plantations, and those of Mr. John and Mr. Frederick Moir at Mandala, and of the Brothers Buchanan at Zomba. And, further, if he desires to know what the milk of human kindness is, let him time his attack of fever so that haply it may coincide with his visit to either of these centres of self-denying goodness and hospitality.

II.

THE EAST AFRICAN LAKE COUNTRY.

LAKES SHIRWA AND NYASSA.

SOMEWHERE in the Shiré Highlands, in 1859, Livingstone saw a large lake—Lake Shirwa—which is still almost unknown. It lies away to the East, and is bounded by a range of mountains whose lofty summits are visible from the hills round Blantyre. Thinking it might be a useful initiation to African travel if I devoted a short time to its exploration, I set off one morning accompanied by two members of the Blantyre staff and a small retinue of natives. Steering across country in the direction in which it lay, we found, two days before seeing the actual water, that we were already on the ancient bed of the lake. Though now clothed with forest, the whole district has obviously been under water at a comparatively recent period, and the shores of Lake Shirwa probably reached at one time to within a few miles of Blantyre itself. On reaching the lake a very aged female chief came to see us, and told us how, long, long ago, a white man came to her village and gave her a present of cloth. Of the white man, who must have been Livingstone, she spoke very kindly; and, indeed, wherever David Livingstone's footsteps are crossed in Africa the fragrance of his memory seems to remain.

The waters of Shirwa are brackish to the taste, and undrinkable; but the saltness must have a peculiar charm for game, for nowhere else in Africa did I see such splendid herds of the larger animals as here. The zebra was especially abundant; and so unaccustomed to be disturbed are these creatures,

that with a little care one could watch their movements safely within a very few yards. It may seem
unorthodox to say so, but I do not know if among
the larger animals there is anything handsomer in
creation than the zebra. At close quarters his striped
coat is all but as fine as the tiger's, while the form
and movement of his body are in every way nobler.
The gait certainly, is not to be compared for grace-
fulness with that of the many species of antelope and
deer who nibble the grass beside him, and one can
never quite forget that scientifically he is an ass ;
but taking him all in all, this fleet and beautiful
animal ought to have a higher place in the regard of
man than he has yet received.

We were much surprised, considering that this
region is almost uninhabited, to discover near the
lake shore a native path so beaten, and so recently
beaten by multitudes of human feet, that it could
only represent some trunk route through the continent. Following it for a few miles, we soon discovered
its function. It was one of the great slave routes
through Africa. Signs of the horrid traffic soon
became visible on every side ; and from symmetrical
arrangements of small piles of stones and freshly-cut
twigs, planted semaphore-wise upon the path, our
native guides made out that a slave-caravan was
actually passing at the time. We were, in fact,
between two portions of it, the stones and twigs
being telegraphic signals between front and rear.
Our natives seemed much alarmed at this discovery,
and refused to proceed unless we promised not to
interfere—a proceeding which, had we attempted it,
would simply have meant murder for ourselves and
slavery for them. Next day, from a hill-top, we saw
the slave encampment far below, and the ghastly
procession marshalling for its march to the distant
coast, which many of the hundreds who composed it
would never reach alive.

Talking of native footpaths leads me to turn aside

for a moment to explain to the uninitiated the true mode of African travel. In spite of all the books that have been lavished upon us by our great explorers, few people seem to have any accurate understanding of this most simple process. Some have the impression that everything is done in bullock-wagons—an idea borrowed from the Cape, but hopelessly inapplicable to Central Africa, where a wheel at present would be as great a novelty as a polar bear. Others at the opposite extreme suppose that the explorer works along solely by compass, making a beeline for his destination, and steering his caravan through the trackless wilderness like a ship at sea. Now it may be a surprise to the unenlightened to learn that probably no explorer in forcing his passage through Africa has ever, for more than a few days at a time, been off some beaten track. Probably no country in the world, civilized or uncivilized, is better supplied with paths than this unmapped continent. Every village is connected with some other village, every tribe with the next tribe, every state with its neighbor, and therefore with all the rest. The explorer's business is simply to select from this network of tracks, keep a general direction, and hold on his way. Let him begin at Zanzibar, plant his foot on a native footpath, and set his face towards Tanganyika. In eight months he will be there. He has simply to persevere. From village to village he will be handed on, zigzagging it may be sometimes to avoid the impassable barriers of nature or the rarer perils of hostile tribes, but never taking to the woods, never guided solely by the stars, never in fact leaving a beaten track, till hundreds and hundreds of miles are between him and the sea, and his interminable footpath ends with a canoe, on the shores of Tanganyika. Crossing the lake, landing near some native village, he picks up the thread once more. Again he plods on and on, now on foot, now by canoe, but always keeping his line of villages, until one day

suddenly he sniffs the sea-breeze again, and his faithful foot-wide guide lands him on the Atlantic sea-
board.

Nor is there any art in finding out these successive
villages with their intercommunicating links. He
must find them out. A whole army of guides, serv-
ants, carriers, soldiers and camp-followers accompany
him in his march, and this nondescript regiment must
be fed. Indian corn, cassava, mawere, beans, and bananas—these do not grow wild even in Africa. Every
meal has to be bought and paid for in cloth and beads;
and scarcely three days can pass without a call having
to be made at some village where the necessary supplies can be obtained. A caravan, as a rule, must live
from hand to mouth, and its march becomes simply a
regulated procession through a chain of markets.
Not, however, that there are any real markets—there
are neither bazaars nor stores in native Africa. Thousands of the villages through which the traveller eats
his way may never have victualled a caravan before.
But, with the chief's consent, which is usually easily
purchased for a showy present, the villages unlock
their larders, the women flock to the grinding stones,
and basketfuls of food are swiftly exchanged for unknown equivalents in beads and calico.

The native tracks which I have just described are
the same in character all over Africa. They are
veritable footpaths, never over a foot in breadth,
beaten as hard as adamant, and rutted beneath the
level of the forest bed by centuries of native traffic.
As a rule these footpaths, are marvellously direct.
Like the roads of the old Romans, they run straight
on through everything, ridge and mountain and valley,
never shying at obstacles, nor anywhere turning aside
to breathe. Yet within this general straightforwardness there is a singular eccentricity and indirectness in
detail. Although the African footpath is on the
whole a bee-line, no fifty yards of it are ever straight.
And the reason is not far to seek. If a stone is

encountered no native will ever think of removing it.
Why should he? It is easier to walk round it. The
next man who comes that way will do the same. He
knows that a hundred men are following him; he
looks at the stone; a moment, and it might be un-
earthed and tossed aside, but no; he also holds on his
way. It is not that he resents the trouble, it is the
idea that is wanting. It would no more occur to him
that that stone was a displaceable object, and that for
the general weal he might displace it, than that its
feldspar was of the orthoclase variety. Generations
and generations of men have passed that stone, and
it still waits for a man with an altruistic idea. But
it would be a very stony country indeed—and Africa
is far from stony—that would wholly account for the
aggravating obliqueness and indecision of the African
footpath. Probably each four miles, on an average
path, is spun out by an infinite series of minor
sinuosities, to five or six. Now these deflections are
not meaningless. Each has some history—a history
dating back, perhaps, a thousand years, but to which
all clue has centuries ago been lost. The leading
cause, probably, is fallen trees. When a tree falls
across a path no man ever removes it. As in the case of
the stone, the native goes round it. It is too green to
burn in his hut; before it is dry, and the white ants
have eaten it, the new detour has become part and
parcel of the path. The smaller irregularities, on the
other hand, represent the trees and stumps of the
primeval forest where the track was made at first.
But whatever the cause, it is certain that for persist-
ent straightforwardness in the general, and utter
vacillation and irresolution in the particular, the African roads are unique in engineering.

Though one of the smaller African lakes, Shirwa
is probably larger than all the lakes of Great Britain
put together. With the splendid environment of
mountains on three of its sides, softened and distanced
by perpetual summer haze, it reminds one somewhat

of the Great Salt Lake simmering in a July sun. We pitched our tent for a day or two on its western shore among a harmless and surprised people who had never gazed on the pallid countenances of Englishmen before. Owing to the ravages of the slaver the people of Shirwa are few, scattered and poor, and live in abiding terror. The densest population is to be found on the small island, heavily timbered with baobabs, which forms a picturesque feature of the northern end. These Wa-Nyassa, or people of the lake, as they call themselves, have been driven here by fear, and they rarely leave their Lake–Dwelling unless under cover of night. Even then they are liable to capture by any man of a stronger tribe who happens to meet them, and numbers who have been kidnapped in this way are to be found in the villages of neighboring chiefs. This is an amenity of existence in Africa that strikes one as very terrible. It is impossible for those at home to understand how literally savage man is a chattel, and how much his life is spent in the mere safeguarding of his main asset, *i. e.*, himself. There are actually districts in Africa where *three* natives cannot be sent a message in case two should combine and sell the third before they return.

After some time spent in the Lake Shirwa and Shiré districts, I set out for the Upper Shiré and Lake Nyassa. Two short days' walk from the settlement at Blantyre brings one once more to the banks of the Shiré. Here I found waiting the famous little *Ilala*, a tiny steamer, little bigger than a large steam launch. It belonged originally to the missionaries on Lake Nyassa, and was carried here a few years ago from England in seven hundred pieces, and bolted together on the river bank. No chapter in romance is more interesting than the story of the pioneer voyage of the *Ilala*, as it sailed away for the first time towards the unknown waters of Nyassa. No keel had ever broken the surface of this mighty lake before, and the wonderment of the natives as the Big Canoe hissed past their villages is described by those who witnessed it as a spectacle of indescribable interest. The *Ilala* is named, of course, after the village where David Livingstone breathed his last. It indicates the heroic mission of the little ship—to take up the work of Civilization and Christianity where the great explorer left it. The *Ilala* now plies at intervals between the Upper Shiré—above the cataracts—and the shores of Lake Nyassa, carrying supplies to the handful of missionaries settled on the western shore. Though commanded by a white man, the work on board is entirely done by natives from the locality. The confidence of the black people once gained, no great difficulty seems to have been found in getting volunteers enough for this novel employment. Singularly enough, while deck hands are often only enlisted after some persuasion, the competition for the office of fireman—a disagreeable post at any time, but in the tropical heat the last to be coveted—is so keen that any number of natives are at all times ready to be frizzled in the stokehole. Instead of avoiding heat, the African native every·where courts it. His nature expands and revels in it; while a breath of cold on a mountain slope, or a sudden shower of rain, transforms him instantly into a most woebegone object.

After leaving Matope, just above the Murchison cataracts, the *Ilala* steams for a couple of days in the river before Lake Nyassa is reached. The valley throughout this length is very broad, bounded on either side by distant mountains which at an earlier period probably formed the shores of a larger Lake Nyassa. The fact that Lake Nyassa is silting up at its southern end becomes more apparent as one nears the lake, for here one finds a considerable expanse already cut off from the larger portion, and forming a separate sheet of water. The smaller lake is Lake Pomalombe, and it is already so shallow that in the dry season the *Ilala's* screw stirs the gray mud at the bottom. The friendship of the few villages along the bank is secured by an occasional present; although the relations between some of them and the Big Canoe are at times a little strained, and in bad humors doubtless they would send it to the bottom if they dared. It is to be remembered that this whole region is as yet altogether beyond the limits, and almost beyond the knowledge of civilization, and few white men have ever been in the country, except the few agents connected with the Lakes Company and the Missions. Beyond an occasional barter of cloth or beads for firewood and food, the *Ilala* has no dealings with the tribes on the Upper Shiré, and at present they are about as much affected by the passing to and fro of the white man's steamer as are the inhabitants of Kensington by an occasional wildfowl making for Regent's Park. One is apt to conclude, from the mere presence of such a thing as a steamer in Central Africa, that the country through which it is passing must be in some sense civilized, and the hourly reminders to the contrary which one receives on the spot are among the most startling experiences of the traveller. It is almost impossible for him to believe, as he watches the native life from the cabin of the *Ilala*, that these people are altogether uncivilized; just as it is impossible for him to believe that that lurch a moment ago was caused by the little craft bumping against a submerged hippopotamus. A steel ship, London built, steaming six knots ahead; and grass huts, nude natives, and a hippopotamus—the ideas refuse to assort themselves, and one lives in a perpetual state of bewilderment and interrogation.

It was a brilliant summer morning when the *Ilala* steamed into Lake Nyassa, and in a few hours we were at anchor in the little bay at Livingstonia. My first impression of this famous mission-station certainly will never be forgotten. Magnificent

mountains of granite, green to the summit with
forest, encircled it, and on the silver sand of a still
smaller bay stood the small row of trim white cottages.
A neat path through a small garden led up to the
settlement, and I approached the largest house and
entered.   It was the Livingstonia manse—the head
missionary's house.   It was spotlessly clean ; English
furniture was in the room, a medicine chest, familiar-
looking dishes were in the cupboards, books lying
about, but there was no missionary in it.   I went to
the next house—it was the school, the benches were
there and the blackboard, but there were no scholars
and no teacher.   I passed to the next, it was the
blacksmith shop ; there were the tools and the
anvil, but there was no blacksmith.   And so on to
the next, and the next, all in perfect order, and all
empty.   Then a native approached and led me a few
yards into the forest.   And there among the mimosa
trees, under a huge granite mountain, were four or
five graves.   These were the missionaries.
    I spent a day or two in the solemn shadow of
that deserted manse.   It is one of the loveliest spots
in the world ; and it was hard to believe, sitting
under the tamarind trees by the quiet lake shore,
that the pestilence which wasteth at midnight had
made this beautiful spot its home.   A hundred and
fifty miles north, on the same lake-coast, the remnant
of the missionaries have begun their task again, and
there, slowly, against fearful odds, they are carrying
on their work.   Travellers have been pleased to say
unkind things of missionaries.   That they are sometimes right, I will not question.   But I will say of
the Livingstonia missionaries, and of the Blantyre
missionaries, and count it an honor to say it, that
they are brave, efficient, single-hearted men, who
need our sympathy more than we know, and are
equally above our criticism and our praise.
    Malarial fever is the one sad certainty which every
African traveller must face.   For months he may

escape, but its finger is upon him, and well for him
if he has a friend near when it finally overtakes him.
It is preceded for weeks, or even for a month or two,
by unaccountable irritability, depression and weari-
ness. On the march with his men he has scarcely
started when he sighs for the noon-day rest. Putting
it down to mere laziness, he goads himself on by
draughts from the water-bottle, and totters forward a
mile or two more. Next he finds himself skulking
into the forest on the pretext of looking at a specimen, and, when his porters are out of sight, throws
himself under a tree in utter limpness and despair.
Roused by mere shame, hes taggers along the trail,
and as he nears the mid-day camp puts on a spurt
to conceal his defeat, which finishes him for the rest
of the day. This is a good place for specimens he
tells the men—the tent may be pitched for the night.
This goes on day after day till the crash comes—
first cold and pain, then heat and pain, then every
kind of pain, and every degree of heat, then delirium,
then the life-and-death struggle. He rises, if he
does rise, a shadow ; and slowly accumulates strength
for the next attack, which he knows too well will
not disappoint him. No one has ever yet got to
the bottom of African fever. Its geographical distribution is still unmapped, but generally it prevails
over the whole east and west coasts within the
tropical limit, along all the river-courses, on the
shores of the inland lakes, and in all low-lying and
marshy districts. The higher plateaux, presumably,
are comparatively free from it, but in order to reach
these, malarious districts of greater or smaller area
have to be traversed. There the system becomes
saturated with fever, which often develops long after
the infected region is left behind. The known facts
with regard to African fever are these : First, it is
connected in some way with drying-up water and
decaying vegetation, though how the germs develop,
or what they are, is unknown. Second, natives

suffer from fever equally with Europeans, and this more particularly in changing from district to district and from altitude to altitude. Thus, in marching over the Tanganyika plateau, four or five of my native carriers were down with fever, although their homes were only two or three hundred miles off, before I had even a touch of it. Third, quinine is the great and almost the sole remedy ; and, fourth, no European ever escapes it.

The really appalling mortality of Europeans is a fact with which all who have any idea of casting in their lot with Africa should seriously reckon. None but those who have been on the spot, or have followed closely the inner history of African exploration and missionary work can appreciate the gravity of the situation. The malaria spares no man ; the strong fall as the weak ; no number of precautions can provide against it ; no kind of care can do more than make the attacks less frequent ; no prediction can be made beforehand as to which regions are haunted by it and which are safe. It is not the least ghastly feature of this invisible plague that the only known scientific test for it at present is a human life. That test has been applied in the Congo region already with a recklessness which the sober judgment can only characterize as criminal. It is a small matter that men should throw away their lives, in hundreds, if need be, for a holy cause ; but it is not a small matter that man after man, in long and in fatal succession, should seek to overleap what is plainly a barrier of Nature. And science has a duty in pointing out that no devotion or enthusiasm can give any man a charmed life, and that those who work for the highest ends will best attain them in humble obedience to the common laws. Transcendentally, this may be denied ; the warning finger may be despised as the hand of the coward and the profane. But the fact remains—the fact of an awful chain of English graves stretching across Africa.

This is not spoken, nevertheless, to discourage missionary enterprise. It is only said to regulate it.

To the head of Lake Nyassa in a little steam yacht is quite a sea-voyage. What with heavy seas, and head-winds, and stopping to wood, and lying-to at nights, it takes longer time than going from England to America. The lake is begirt with mountains, and storms are so incessant and so furious that Livingstone actually christened Nyassa the "Lake of Storms." The motion on anchoring at night was generally so unpleasant that one preferred then to be set on shore. My men—for I had already begun to pick up my caravan whenever I could find a native willing to go—would kindle fires all round to keep off beasts of prey, and we slept in peace upon the soft lake sand.

Instead of being one hundred and fifty miles long, as first supposed, Lake Nyassa is now known to have a length of three hundred and fifty miles, and a breadth varying from sixteen to sixty miles. It occupies a gigantic trough of granite and gneiss, the profoundly deep water standing at a level of sixteen hundred feet above the sea, with the mountains rising all around it, and sometimes sheer above it, to a height of one, two, three, and four thousand feet. The mountains along the west coast form an almost unbroken chain, while the north-east and north are enclosed by the vast range of the Livingstone Mountains. The anchorages on the lake are neither so numerous nor so sheltered as might be wished, but the *Ilala* has picked out some fair harbors on the west coast, and about half as many are already known on the east.

I only visited one native village on the lake, and I should hope there are none others like it—indeed it was quite exceptional for Africa. I tumbled into it early one morning, out of the *Ilala's* dingy, and lost myself at once in an endless labyrinth of reeking huts. Its filth was indescribable, and I met stricken men, at the acute stage of smallpox, wandering about the place at every turn, as if infection were a thing unknown. The chief is the greatest slaver and the worst villain on the lake, and impaled upon poles all round his lodge, their ghastly faces shrivelling in the sun, I counted forty human heads.

This village was not African, however. It was Arab. The native villages on Nyassa are rarely so large, seldom so compact, and never so dirty. Everywhere they straggle along the shore and through the forest, and altogether there must be many hundreds of them scattered about the lake. On the western shore alone there are at least fifteen different tribes, speaking as many different languages, and each of them with dialects innumerable.

The bright spot on Lake Nyassa is Bandawé, the present headquarters of the Scotch Livingstonia Mission. The phrase "headquarters of a mission" suggests to the home Christian a street and a square, with its overshadowing church; a decent graveyard; and a reverent community in its Sunday clothes. But Bandawé is only a lodge or two in a vast wilderness, and the swarthy worshippers flock to the seatless chapel on M'lunga's day dressed mostly in bows and arrows. The said chapel, nevertheless, is as great an achievement in its way as Cologne Cathedral, and its worshippers are quite as much interested, and some of them at least to quite as much purpose. In reality no words can be a fit witness here to the impression made by Dr. Laws, Mrs. Laws, and their few helpers, upon this singular and apparently intractable material. A visit to Bandawé is a great moral lesson. And I cherish no more sacred memory of my life than that of a communion service in the little Bandawé chapel, when the sacramental cup was handed to me by the bare black arm of a native communicant —a communicant whose life, tested afterwards in many an hour of trial with me on the Tanganyika plateau, gave him perhaps a better right to be there than any of us.

III.

THE HEART OF AFRICA.

THE COUNTRY AND ITS PEOPLE.

WE are now far enough into the interior to form some general idea of the aspect of the heart of Africa. I shall not attempt to picture any particular spot. The description about to be given applies generally to Shirwa, the Shiré Highlands, Nyassa, and the Nyassa-Tanganyika plateau—regions which together make up one of the great lobes of the heart of Africa.

Nothing could more wildly misrepresent the reality than the idea of one's school days that the heart of Africa is a desert. Africa rises from its three environing oceans in three great tiers, and the general physical geography of these has been already sketched —first, a coast-line, low and deadly; farther in, a plateau the height of the Scottish Grampians; farther in still, a higher plateau, covering the country for thousands of miles with mountain and valley. Now fill in this sketch, and you have Africa before you. Cover the coast belt with rank yellow grass, dot here and there a palm; scatter through it a few demoralized villages; and stock it with the leopard, the hyena, the crocodile, and the hippopotamus. Clothe the mountainous plateaux next—both of them—with endless forest,—not grand umbrageous forest like the forests of South America, nor matted jungle like the forests of India, but with thin, rather weak forest,—with forest of low trees, whose half-grown trunks and scanty leaves offer no shade from the tropical sun. Nor is there anything in these trees to the casual eye to remind you that you are in the tropics. Here and there one comes upon a borassus

or fan-palm, a candelabra-like euphorbia, a mimosa
aflame with color, or a sepulchral baobab. A close
inspection also will discover curious creepers and
climbers ; and among the branches strange orchids
hide their eccentric flowers. But the outward type
of tree is the same as we have at home—trees resembling the ash, the beech, and the elm, only
seldom so large, except by the streams, and never so
beautiful.[1] Day after day you may wander through
these forests with nothing except the climate to
remind you where you are. The beasts, to be sure,
are different, but unless you watch for them you will
seldom see any ; the birds are different, but you rarely
hear them ; and as for the rocks, they are our own
familiar gneisses and granites, with honest basalt-
dykes boring through them, and leopard-skin lichens
staining their weathered sides. Thousands and thousands of miles, then, of vast thin forest, shadeless,
trackless, voiceless—forest in mountain and forest
in plain—this is East Central Africa.

The indiscriminate praise formerly lavished on tropical vegetation has received many shocks from recent
travellers. In Kaffirland, South Africa, I have seen
one or two forests fine enough to justify the enthusiasm of armchair word-painters of the tropics ;
but so far as the central plateau is concerned, the
careful judgment of Mr. Alfred Russel Wallace re-
specting the equatorial belt in general—a judgment
which has at once sobered all modern descriptions of
tropical lands, and made imaginative people more
content to stay at home—applies almost to this
whole area. The fairy labyrinth of ferns and palms,
the festoons of climbing plants blocking the paths and
scenting the forests with their resplendent flowers,
the gorgeous clouds of insects, the gaily-plumaged

---

[1] The more important of these trees are—*Napaca Kirkii,
Brachystegia longifolia, Vitex umbrosa, Erythrina speciosa, Ficus
sycamorus, Khaya senegalensis, Nuxia congesta, Parinarium
mobola,* and *Erythrophlœum guineensis.*

birds, the paroquets, the monkey swinging from his trapeze in the shaded bowers—these are unknown to Africa. Once a week you will see a palm ; once in three months the monkey will cross your path ; the flowers on the whole are few ; the trees are poor ; and, to be honest, though the endless forest-clad mountains have a sublimity of their own, and though there are tropical bits along some of the mountain-streams of exquisite beauty, nowhere is there anything in grace and sweetness and strength to compare with a Highland glen. For the most part of the year these forests are jaded and sun-stricken, carpeted with no moss or alchemylla or scented woodruff, the bare trunks frescoed with few lichens, their motionless and unrefreshed leaves drooping sullenly from their sapless boughs. Flowers there are, small and great, in endless variety ; but there is no display of flowers, no gorgeous show of blossom in the mass, as when the blazing gorse and heather bloom at home. The dazzling glare of the sun in the torrid zone has perhaps something to do with this want of color-effect in tropical nature ; for there is always about ten minutes just after sunset, when the whole tone of the landscape changes like magic, and a singular beauty steals over the scene. This is the sweetest moment of the African day, and night hides only too swiftly the homelike softness and repose so strangely grateful to the over-stimulated eye.

Hidden away in these endless forests, like birds' nests in a wood, in terror of one another, and of their common foe, the slaver, are small native villages ; and here in his virgin simplicity dwells the primeval man, without clothes, without civilization, without learning, without religion— the genuine child of nature, thoughtless, careless, and contented. This man is apparently quite happy ; he has practically no wants. One stick, pointed, makes him a spear ; two sticks rubbed together make him a fire ; fifty sticks tied together make him a house. The bark

he peels from them makes his clothes; the fruits
which hang on them form his food. It is perfectly
astonishing when one thinks of it what nature can
do for the animal-man, to see with what small capital
after all a human being can get through the world.
I once saw an African buried. According to the
custom of his tribe, his entire earthly possessions—
and he was an average commoner—were buried with
him. Into the grave, after the body, was lowered
the dead man's pipe, then a rough knife, then a mud
bowl, and last his bow and arrows—the bow string
cut through the middle, a touching symbol that its
work was done. This was all. Four items, as an
auctioneer would say, were the whole belongings for
half a century of this human being. No man knows
what a man is till he has seen what a man can be
without, and be withal a man. That is to say, no
man knows how great man is till he has seen how
small he has been once.

The African is often blamed for being lazy, but
it is a misuse of words. He does not need to work;
with so bountiful a nature round him it would be
gratuitous to work. And his indolence, therefore, as
it is called, is just as much a part of himself as his
flat nose, and as little blameworthy as slowness in
a tortoise. The fact is, Africa is a nation of the unemployed.

This completeness, however, will be a sad drawback to development. Already it is found difficult
to create new wants; and when labor is required,
and you have already paid your man a yard of calico
and a string of beads, you have nothing in your
possession to bribe him to another hand's turn.
Nothing almost that you have would be the slightest
use to him. Among the presents which I took for
chiefs, I was innocent enough to include a watch.
I might as well have taken a grand piano. For
months I never looked at my own watch in that
land of sunshine. Besides, the mere idea of time has

scarcely yet penetrated the African mind, and forms
no element whatever in his calculations. I wanted
on one occasion to catch the little steamer on the
Shiré, and pleaded this as an excuse to a rather
powerful chief, whom it would have been dangerous
to quarrel with, and who would not let me leave his
village. The man merely stared. The idea of any
one being in a hurry was not only preposterous but
inconceivable, and I might as well have urged as
my reason for wishing away that the angles of a
triangle are equal to two right angles.

This difference in ideas is the real obstacle to
African travelling, and it raises all sorts of problems
in one's mind as to the nature of ideas themselves.
I often wished I could get inside an African for an
afternoon, and just see how he looked at things; for
I am sure our worlds are as different as the color of
our skins.

Talking of skins, I may observe in passing that
the highland African is not a negro, nor is his skin
black. It is a deep full-toned brown, something like
the color of a good cigar. The whole surface is
diced with a delicate pattern, which gives it great
richness and beauty, and I often thought how effective a row of books would be bound in native-
morocco.

No one knows exactly who these people are.
They belong, of course, to the great Bantu race ; but
their origin is obscure, their tribal boundaries are
unmapped, even their names are unknown, and their
languages—for they are many—are unintelligible.
A fine-looking people, quiet and domestic, their life-
history from the cradle to the grave is of the utmost
simplicity. Too ill armed to hunt, they live all but
exclusively on a vegetable diet. A small part of the
year they depend, like the monkeys, upon wild fruits
and herbs ; but the staple food is a small tasteless
millet-seed which they grow in gardens, crush in a
mortar, and stir with water into a thick porridge.

40 *TROPICAL AFRICA.*

Twice a day, nearly all the year round, each man stuffs himself with this coarse and tasteless dough, shoveling it into his mouth in handfuls, and consuming at a sitting a pile the size of an ant-heap. His one occupation is to grow this millet, and his gardening is a curiosity. Selecting a spot in the forest, he climbs a tree, and with a small home-made axe lops off the branches one by one. He then wades through the litter to the next tree, and hacks it to pieces also, leaving the trunk standing erect. Upon all the trees within a circle of thirty or forty yards diameter his axe works similar havoc, till the ground stands breast-high in leaves and branches. Next, the whole is set on fire and burned to ashes. Then, when the first rains moisten the hard ground and wash the fertile chemical constituents of the ash into the soil, he attacks it with his hoe, drops in a few handfuls of millet, and the year's work is over. But a few weeks off and on are required for these operations, and he may then go to sleep till the rains are over, assured of a crop which never fails, which is never poor, and which will last him till the rains return again.

Between the acts he does nothing but lounge and sleep; his wife, or wives, are the millers and bakers; they work hard to prepare his food, and are rewarded by having to take their own meals apart, for no African would ever demean himself by eating with a woman. I have tried to think of something else that these people habitually do, but their vacuous life leaves nothing more to tell.

Apart from eating, their sole occupation is to talk, and this they do unceasingly, emphasizing their words with a marvellous wealth of gesticulation. Talking, indeed, is an art here—the art it must once have been in Europe before the newspaper drove it out of fashion. The native voices are sometimes highly musical, though in the strict sense the people have no notion whatever of singing; and the languages themselves are full of melody. Every word, like the

Italian, ends in a vowel, and when well spoken they are exceedingly effective and full of character.

Notwithstanding their rudimentary estate, the people of Africa have the beginnings of all the more characteristic things that make up the life of civilized man. They have a national amusement, the dance; a national musical instrument, the drum; a national drink, *pombé;* a national religion, the fear of evil spirits. Their chamber of justice is a council of head-men or chiefs; their court of appeal, the *muavi*, or poison cup. No new thing is found here that is not in some form in modern civilization; no new thing in civilization but has its embryo and prophecy in the simpler life of these primitive tribes. To the igno-rant these men are animals; but the eye of evolution looks on them with a kindlier and more instructed sense. They are what we were once; possibly they may become what we are now.

What, then, is to become of this strange people and their land? With the glowing figures of a very distinguished traveller in our minds, are we to expect that the Shiré and Congo routes have but to be con-nected with New York and Manchester to cause at once a revolution among the people of Africa and in the commerce of the world? We hear two criticisms upon that subject. One complains that while Mr. Stanley emphasizes in the most convincing way the thousands of miles of cloth the African is waiting to receive from Europe, he is all but silent as to what Europe is to get in return. A second remark is that Africa has nothing to give in return, and never will have.

The facts of the case briefly, as it seems to me, are these :—

First, The only thing of value the interior of Africa produces at present in any quantity is ivory. There is still, undoubtedly, a supply of this precious material in the country—a supply which may last yet for fifteen or twenty years. But it is well to frame future calculation on the certainty of this abnormal source of wealth ceasing, as it must do, in the immediate future.

Second, Africa already produces in a wild state a number of vegetable and other products of considerable commercial value; and although the soil can only be said to be of average fertility, there is practically no limit to the extent to which these could be developed.

Wild indigo—the true *indigofera tinctoria* is already growing on the hills of the interior. The Londolphia, an indiarubber-bearing creeper, is to be seen on most of the watercourses; and a variety of the *Ficus elastica*, the well-known rubber plant, abounds on Lake Nyassa. The orchilla weed is common. The castor-oil plant, ginger, and other spices, the tobacco-plant, the cotton-plant, and many fibre-yielding grasses, are also found; and oil-seeds of every variety and in endless quantity are grown by the natives for local use.

The fatal drawback, meantime, to the further development of these comparatively invaluable products is the transit, carriage to the coast from Nyassa or Tanganyika being almost prohibitive. Up till very recently only two native products have ever been exported from this region—indiarubber and beeswax, and these in but trifling quantity. But there is no reason why these products should not be largely developed, and freights must become lower and lower every year. In addition to the plants named, the soil of Central Africa is undoubtedly adapted for growing coffee; and the Cinchona would probably flourish well on the higher grounds of the Tanganyika plateau.

I must not omit to mention in this connection that an attempt is now being made, and so far with marked success, to form actual plantations in the interior of Africa; and the result of the experiment ought to be watched with exceptional interest. Mr. Moir, on

behalf of the African Lakes Company, and the Brothers
Buchanan on their own account, and also Mr. Scott,
with remarkable industry and enterprise have each
formed at Blantyre a coffee plantation of considerable size. The plants, when I saw them, were still
young, but very healthy and promising, and already
a first crop of fine coffee-berries hung from the trees,
and has since been marketed. These same gentlemen
have also grown heavy crops of wheat; and Mr.
Buchanan has succeeded well with sugar-cane, potatoes and other English vegetables. The manual work
here has been entirely done by natives ; and an immense saving to resident Europeans will be effected
when the interior is able to provide its own food
supplies, for at present wheat, coffee, and sugar, have
all to be imported from home.

With so satisfactory an account of the possibilities
of the country, the only question that remains is this
—Can the African native really be taught to work ?

This question I answer unhesitatingly in the affirm-
ative. I have described Africa as a nation of the
unemployed. But the sole reason for the current impression that the African is an incorrigible idler is
that at present there is really nothing for him to do.
But that he can work and will work when the opportunity and inducement offer has been proved by
experiment. The coast native, as all must testify who
have seen him in the harbor of Zanzibar, Mozambique,
Delagoa Bay, Natal, or the other eastern ports, is,
with all allowances, a splendid worker; and though
the experiment has seldom been tried in the interior,
it is well known that the capacity is there, and
wherever encouraged yields results beyond all expec-
tation. Probably the severest test to which the native
of Central Africa has ever been put is the construction of the Stevenson road, between Lakes Nyassa
and Tanganyika. Forty-six miles of that road—
probably the only thing of the kind in Central Africa
—have already been made entirely by native labor,

and the work could not have been better done had it
been executed by English navvies. I have watched
by the day a party of seventy natives working at a
cutting upon that road. Till three or four years ago
none of them had ever looked upon a white man ;
nor, till a few months previously, had one of them
seen a spade, a pickaxe, or a crowbar. Yet these
savages handled their tools to such purpose that, with
only a single European superintendent, they have
made a road, full of difficult cuttings and gradients,
which would not disgrace a railway contractor at
home. The workmen keep regular hours—six in the
morning till five at night, with a rest at mid-day—
work steadily, continuously, willingly, and above all,
merrily. This goes on, observe, in the heart of the
tropics, almost under the equator itself, where the
white man's energy evaporates, and leaves him so
limp that he cannot even be an example to his men.
This goes on too without any compulsion ; the natives
flock from far and near, sometimes from long distances, to try this new sensation of work. These
men are not slaves, but volunteers ; and though they
are paid by the fortnight, many will remain at their
post the whole season through. The only bribe for
all this work is a yard or two of calico per week per
man ; so that it seems to me one of the greatest
problems of the future of Africa is here solved. In
capacity the African is fit to work, in inclination he
is willing to work, and in actual experiment he has
done it ; so that with capital enlisted and wise heads
to direct these energies, with considerate employers
who will remember that these men are but children,
this vast nation of the unemployed may yet be added
to the slowly growing list of the world's producers.

Africa at this moment has an impossible access, a
perilous climate, a penniless people, an undeveloped
soil. So once had England. It may never be done ;
other laws may operate, unforeseen factors may interfere ; but there is nothing in the soil, the products,

the climate, or the people of Africa, to forbid its
joining even at this late day in the great march of
civilization.

IV.

THE HEART-DISEASE OF AFRICA.

ITS PATHOLOGY AND CURE.

THE life of the native African is not all idyll. It
is darkened by a tragedy whose terrors are unknown
to any other people under heaven. Of its mild
domestic slavery I do not speak, nor of its revolting
witchcraft, nor of its endless quarrels and frequent
tribal wars. These minor evils are lost in the shadow
of a great and national wrong. Among these simple
and unprotected tribes, Arabs—uninvited strangers
of another race and nature—pour in from the North
and East, with the deliberate purpose of making this
paradise a hell. It seems the awful destiny of this
homeless people to spend their lives in breaking up
the homes of others. Wherever they go in Africa
the followers of Islam are the destroyers of peace, the
breakers up of the patriarchal life, the dissolvers of
the family tie. Already they hold the whole Continent under one reign of terror. They have effected
this in virtue of one thing—they possess firearms;
and they do it for one object—ivory and slaves, for
these two are one. The slaves are needed to buy
ivory with; then more slaves have to be stolen to
carry it. So living man himself has become the
commercial currency of Africa. He is locomotive, he
is easily acquired, he is immediately negotiable.

Arab encampments for carrying on a wholesale
trade in this terrible commodity are now established
all over the heart of Africa. They are usually connected with wealthy Arab traders at Zanzibar and

other places on the coast, and communication is kept up by caravans which pass, at long intervals, from one to the other. Being always large and well supplied with the material of war, these caravans have at their mercy the feeble and divided native tribes through which they pass, and their trail across the Continent is darkened with every aggravation of tyranny and crime. They come upon the scene suddenly; they stay only long enough to secure their end, and disappear only to return when a new crop has arisen which is worth the reaping.

Sometimes these Arab traders will actually settle for a year or two in the heart of some quiet community in the remote interior. They pretend perfect friendship; they molest no one; they barter honestly. They plant the seeds of their favorite vegetables and fruits—the Arab always carries seeds with him—as if they meant to stay for ever. Meantime they buy ivory, tusk after tusk, until great piles of it are buried beneath their huts and all their barter-goods are gone. Then one day, suddenly, the inevitable quarrel is picked. And then follows a wholesale massacre. Enough only are spared from the slaughter to carry the ivory to the coast; the grass-huts of the villages are set on fire; the Arabs strike camp; and the slave-march, worse than death, begins.

This last act in the drama, the slave-march, is the aspect of slavery which, in the past, has chiefly aroused the passions and the sympathy of the outside world, but the greater evil is the demoralization and disintegration of communities by which it is necessarily preceded. It is essential to the traffic that the region drained by the slaver should be kept in perpetual political ferment; that, in order to prevent combination, chief should be pitted against chief; and that the moment any tribe threatened to assume a dominating strength it should either be broken up by the instigation of rebellion among its dependencies, or made a tool of at their expense. The inter-

relation of tribe with tribe is so intricate that it is
impossible to exaggerate the effect of disturbing the
equilibrium at even a single centre. But, like a
river, a slave-caravan has to be fed by innumerable
tributaries all along its course—at first in order to
gather a sufficient volume of human bodies for the
start, and afterwards to replace the frightful loss by
desertion, disablement, and death.

Many at home imagine that the death-knell of
slavery was struck with the events which followed
the death of Livingstone. In the great explorer's
time we heard much of slavery; we were often
appealed to; the Government busied itself; something was really done. But the wail is already forgotten, and England hears little now of the open
sore of the world. But the tragedy I have alluded
to is repeated every year and every month—witness
such recent atrocities as those of the Upper Congo,
the Kassai and Sankaru region described by Wiss-
mann, of the Welle-Inakua district referred to by
Van Gele. It was but yesterday that an explorer,
crossing from Lake Nyassa to Lake Tanganyika,
saw the whole southern. end of Tanganyika peopled
with large and prosperous villages. The next to
follow him found not a solitary human being—
nothing but burned homes and bleaching skeletons.
It was but yesterday—the close of 1887—that the
Arabs at the north end of Lake Nyassa, after destroy-
ing fourteen villages with many of their inhabitants,
pursued the population of one village into a patch
of tall dry grass, set it on fire, surrounded it, and
slew with the bullet and the spear those who crawled
out from the more merciful flames. The Wa-Nkonde
tribe, to which these people belonged, were, until
this event, one of the most prosperous tribes in
East Central Africa. They occupied a country of
exceptional fertility and beauty. Three rivers, which
never failed in the severest drought, run through
their territory, and their crops were the richest and

most varied in the country. They possessed herds
of cattle and goats; they fished in the lake with
nets; they wrought iron into many-patterned spear-
heads with exceptional ingenuity and skill; and that
even artistic taste had begun to develop among
them was evident from the ornamental work upon
their huts, which were themselves unique in Africa
for clever construction and beauty of design. This
people, in short, by their own inherent ability and
the natural resources of their country, were on the
high road to civilization. Now, mark the swift
stages in their decline and fall. Years ago an almost
unnoticed rill from that great Arab stream, which
with noiseless current and ever-changing bed has
never ceased to flow through Africa, trickled into
the country. At first the Arab was there on suffer-
ance; he paid his way. Land was bought from the
Wa-Nkonde chiefs, and their sovereignty acknowledged. The Arab force grew. In time it developed
into a powerful incursion, and the Arabs began
openly to assert themselves. One of their own
number was elevated to the rulership, with the title
of "Sultan of Nkonde." The tension became great,
and finally too severe to last. After innumerable
petty fights the final catastrophe was hurried on,
and after an atrocious carnage the remnant of the
Wa-Nkonde were driven from their fatherland. Such
is the very last chapter in the history of Arab rule in
Africa.

The Germans, the Belgians, the English, and the
Portuguese, are crying out at present for territory in
Central Africa. Meantime humanity is crying out
for some one to administer the country; for some
one to claim it, not by delimiting a frontier-line upon
a map with colored crayons, but by seeing justice
done upon the spot; for some one with a strong arm
and a pitiful heart to break the Arab yoke and keep
these unprotected children free. It has been reserved
for a small company of English gentlemen to arrest

the hand of the raider in the episode I have just described. While Germany covets Nyassa-land, while Portugal claims it, while England has sent a consul there, *without protection,* to safeguard British missionary and trading interests, two agents of the African Lakes Company, two missionaries, the British Consul at Mozambique, with two companions who happened to be in Nyassa-land on scientific work, have, at the risk of their lives, averted further war, and with their own rifles avenged the crime.

But this fortuitous concourse of English rifles cannot be reckoned upon every day ; nor is it the part of the missionary and the trader to play the game of war. The one thing needed for Africa at present is some system of organized protection to the native, and the decisive breaking of the Arab influence throughout the whole interior. These events at Lake Nyassa have brought this subject once more before the civilized world, and I may briefly state the situation as it at present stands.

Five years ago the British cruisers which had been for years engaged in suppressing the slave-trade were tempted to relax their efforts. They had done splendid service. The very sight of the great hull of the *London,* as she rocked in the harbor of Zanzibar, had a pacific influence ; and as the caravans from the interior came and went at intervals of years and found the cruiser's cannon still pointing to their sultan's palace, they carried the fear of England over the length and breadth of Africa. The slave-trade was seriously discouraged, and, so far as the coast traffic was concerned, it was all but completely arrested. What work, up to this point, was done, was well done ; but, after all, only half the task had ever been attempted. It was not enough to stop the sewer at its mouth ; its sources in the heart of Africa should have been sought out and purified. But now that even the menace at Zanzibar no longer threatened the slavers, their work was resumed with re-

doubled energy. The withdrawal of the *London*
was interpreted to mean either that England con-
ceived her work to be done or that she had grown
apathetic and would interfere no more.

The consequences were almost immediately disastrous. A new license to devastate, to murder, and
to enslave, was telegraphed all over Africa, and
speedily found expression, in widely separated parts
of the country, in horrors the details of which can
never be known to the civilized world. The disturb-
ances on Lake Nyassa undoubtedly belong, though
indirectly, to this new category of crime. Already
the Arabs have learned that there is no one now to
take them to task. In one district after another they
have played their game and won; and with ample
power, with absolute immunity from retribution, and
with the sudden creation of a new demand for slaves
in a quarter of which I dare not speak further here,
their offenses can only increase in number and
audacity. It is remarkable in the Wa-Nkonde episode that, for the first time probably in Central
Africa, the Mohammedan defiance to the Christian
power was open and undisguised. Hitherto the
Arab worked in secret. The mere presence of a
white man in the country was sufficient to stay his
hand. On this occasion the Arab not only did not
conceal his doings from the Europeans, nor flee
when he was remonstrated with, but turned and
attacked his monitors. The political significance of
this is plain. It is part of a policy. It is a challenge
to Europe from the whole Mohammedan power.
Europe in Africa is divided; Mohammedanism is
one. No isolated band of Arabs would have ventured upon such a line of action unless they were
perfectly sure of their ground. Nor is there any
reason why they should not be sure of their ground.
Europe is talking much about Africa; it is doing
nothing. This the Arab has discerned. It is one of
the most astounding facts in morals that England

should have kept the Arab at bay so long. But the time of probation is over. And the plain issue is now before the world—Is the Arab or the European henceforth to reign in Africa?

How the European could reign in Africa is a simple problem. The real difficulty is as to who in Europe will do it. Africa is claimed by everybody, and it belongs to nobody. So far as the Nyassa region is concerned, while the Portuguese assert their right to the south and west, scarcely one of them has ever set foot in it: and while the Germans claim the north and east, their pretension is based neither upon right of discovery, right of treaty, right of purchase, right of conquest, nor right of possession, but on the cool audacity of some chartographer in Berlin, who, in delineating a tract of country recognized as German by the London Convention of 1886, allowed his paint-brush to color some tens of thousands of square miles beyond the latitude assigned. To England it is a small matter politically who gets Africa. But it is of moment that those who secure the glory of annexation should not evade the duty of administration. The present condition of Africa is too critical to permit so wholesale a system of absentee landlordism; and it is the duty of England, so far at least as the Nyassa region is concerned, to insist on the various claimants either being true to their assumed responsibilities or abandoning a nominal sovereignty.

It is well known,—it is certain,—that neither Portugal nor Germany will ever administer this region. If they would, the problem would be solved, and England would gladly welcome the release; the release, for, although England has never aided this country with a force of arms, she has for some time known that in some way, direct or indirect, she ought to do it. This country is, in a special sense, the *protegé* of England. Since Livingstone's death the burden of it has never really left her conscience.

The past relation of England to Nyassa-land, and her duty now, will be apparent from the following simple facts :—

Lake Nyassa was discovered by David Livingstone. At that time he was acting as Her Majesty's Consul, and was sent to Africa with a Government Expedition, which was equipped not to perform an exceptional and romantic piece of work, but in accordance with a settled policy on the part of England. "The main object of the Zambesi Expedition," says Livingstone, "as our instructions from Her Majesty's Government explicitly stated, was to extend the knowledge already attained of the geography, and mineral and agricultural resources, of Eastern and Central Africa; to improve our acquaintance with the inhabitants, and to endeavor to engage them to apply themselves to industrial pursuits, and to the cultivation of their lands, with a view to the production of raw material to be exported to England in return for British manufactures; and it was hoped that, by encouraging the natives to occupy themselves in the development of the resources of the country, a considerable advance might be made towards the extinction of the slave-trade, as they would not be long in discovering that the former would eventually be a more certain source of profit than the latter. The Expedition was sent *in accordance with the settled policy of the English Government;* and the Earl of Clarendon being then at the head of the Foreign Office, the Mission was organized under his immediate care. When a change of Government ensued we experienced the same generous countenance and sympathy from the Earl of Malmesbury as we had previously received from Lord Clarendon; and on the accession of Earl Russell to the high office he has so long filled we were always favored with equally ready attention and the same prompt assistance. Thus *the conviction was produced that our work embodied the principles not of any one party, but of the hearts of the statesmen and of the people of England generally."*

Encouraged by this national interest in Africa, the churches of England and Scotland attempted to follow up the work of Livingstone in one at least of its aspects, by sending missionaries into the country. These have already succeeded in establishing themselves in one district after another, and are daily extending in numbers and influence.

In order to perpetuate a scarcely less important branch of the movement initiated by Livingstone, —a department specially sanctioned, as the above extract shows, by the English Government—the African Lakes Company was formed in 1878. Its object was to open up and develop the regions of East Central Africa from the Zambesi to Tanganyika; to make employments for the native peoples, to trade with them honestly, to keep out rum, and, so far as possible, gunpowder and firearms, and to co-operate and strengthen the hands of the missionary. It has already established twelve trading stations, manned by a staff of twenty-five Europeans and many native agents. The *Ilala* on Lake Nyassa belongs to it; and it has just placed a new steamer to supersede the *Lady Nyassa* on the river Shiré. It has succeeded in starting a flourishing coffee plantation in the interior, and new sources of wealth are being gradually introduced. For the first time, on the large scale, it has taught the natives the meaning and the blessings of work. It has acted, to some extent, as a check upon the slave-trade; it has prevented inter-tribal strife, and helped to protect the missionaries in time of war. The African Lakes Company, in short, modest as is the scale on which it works, and, necessarily limited as are its opportunities, has been for years the sole administering hand in this part of Africa. This Company does not exist for gain;—or exists for gain only in the sense that commercial soundness is the only solid basis on

which to build up an institution which can perma-
nently benefit others.   A large amount of private
capital has been expended by this Company; yet,
during all the years it has carried on its noble enterprise, it has re-invested in Africa all that it has taken
from it.

All this British capital, all the capital of the Missions, all these various and not inconsiderable agencies, have been tempted into Africa largely in the
hope that the old policy of England would not only
be continued but extended.   England has never in
theory departed from the position she assumed in the
days of the Zambesi Expedition.   On the contrary,
she has distinctly recognized the relation between
her Government and Africa.   She has continued to
send out British Consuls to be the successors of Livingstone in the Nyassa region.   When the first of
these, Captain Foote, R. N., died in the Shiré Highlands in 1884, the English Government immediately
sent another to take his place.   But this is the last
thing that has been done.   The Consul is there as a
protest that England has still her eye on Africa.   But
Africa needs more than an eye.   And when, as happened the other day, one of Her Majesty's representatives was under Arab fire for five days and nights
on the shores of Lake Nyassa, this was brought home
to us in such practical fashion as to lead to the hope
that some practical measures will now be taken.

I do not presume to bring forward a formal pro-
posal; but two things occur to one as feasible, and
I shall simply name them.   The first is for England,
or Germany, or France, or some one with power and
earnestness, to take a firm and uncompromising stand
at Zanzibar.   Zanzibar, as the Arab capital, is one of
the keys of the situation, and any lesson taught here
would be learned presently by the whole Mohammedan following in the country.

The other key to the situation is the vast and
splendid water-way in the heart of Africa—the Up-

per Shiré, Lake Nyassa, Lake Tanganyika, and the
Great Lakes generally. As a base for military or
patrol operations nothing better could be desired
than these great inland seas. A small steamer upon
each of them—or, to begin with, upon Nyassa and
Tanganyika—with an associated depôt or two of
armed men on the higher and healthier plateaux
which surround them, would keep the whole country
quiet. Only a trifling force of well-drilled men
would be needed for this purpose. They might be
whites, or blacks and whites; they might be Sikhs or
Pathans from India; and the expense is not to be
named considering the magnitude of the results—
the pacification of the entire equatorial region—that
would be achieved. That expense could be borne
by the Missions, but it is not their province to employ the use of force; it could be borne by the Lakes
Company, only they deserve protection from others
rather than that this should be added to the large
debt civilization already owes them; it could be done
by the Free Congo State,—and if no one else is
shamed into doing it, this further labor of love may
fall into its hands. But whether alone, or in co-
operation with the few and overburdened capitalists
of the country, or in conjunction with foreign powers, England will be looked to to take the initiative
with this or a similar scheme.

The barriers in the way of Government action are
only two, and neither is insurmountable. The one is
Portugal, which owns the approaches to the country;
the other is Germany, which has inland interests of
her own. Whether England could proceed in the
face of these two powers would simply depend on
how it was done. As a mere political move such an
occupation of the interior might at once excite alarm
and jealousy. But wearing the aspect of a serious
mission for the good of Africa, instigated not by the
Foreign Office but by the people of England, it is
impossible to believe that the step could either be

misunderstood or opposed. It is time the nations looked upon Africa as something more than a chess-board. And even if it were but a chess-board, the players on every hand are wise enough to know that whatever is honestly done to relieve this suffering continent will react in a hundred ways upon the interests of all who hold territorial rights within it.

A beginning once made, one might not be unduly sanguine in anticipating that the meshes of a pacific and civilizing influence would rapidly spread throughout the country. Already the missionaries are pioneering everywhere, prepared to slay and do their part; and asking no more from the rest of the world than a reasonable guarantee that they should be allowed to live. Already the trading companies are there, from every nationality, and in every direction ready to open up the country, but unable to go on with any confidence or enthusiasm till their isolated interests are linked together and secured in the presence of a common foe. The territories of the various colonies are slowly converging upon the heart of Africa, and to unite them in an informal defensive alliance would not be impossible. With Emin Pasha occupying the field in the north; with the African Lakes Company, the British East African Association, and the German Association, in the east; with the Congo Free State in the west, and British Bechuanaland in the south, a cordon is already thrown around the Great Lakes region, which requires only to have its several parts connected with one another and with central forces on the Lakes, to secure the peace of Africa.

V.

WANDERINGS ON THE NYASSA-TANGANYIKA PLATEAU.

A TRAVELLER'S DIARY.

WITH a glade in the forest for a study, a bale of calico for a table, and the sun vertical and something under a billion centigrade, diary-writing in the tropics is more picturesque than inspiring. To keep a journal, however, next to keeping his scalp, is the one thing for which the consistent traveller will go through fire and water; and the dusky native who carries the faded note-books on the march is taught to regard the sacredness of his office more than if he drove the car of Juggernaut. The contents of these mysterious note-books, nevertheless, however precious to those who write them, are, like the photographs of one's relations, of pallid interest to others, and I have therefore conscientiously denied myself the joy of exhibiting such offspring of the wilderness as I possess to my confiding reader.

But as the diary form has advantages of its own, I make no apology at this stage for transcribing and editing a few rough pages. Better, perhaps, than by a more ordered narrative, they may help others to enter into the traveller's life, and to illustrate what the African traveller sees and hears and does. I shall disregard names, and consecutive dates, and routes. My object is simply to convey some impression of how the world wags in a land unstirred by civilization, and all but untouched by time.

29th September.—Left Karongas, at the north end of Lake Nyassa, at 10.30, with a mongrel retinue of seven Mandalla natives, twelve Bandawé Atongas, six Chingus, and my three faithfuls—Jingo, Moolu, and Seyid. Total twenty-eight. Not one of my men could speak a word of English. They belonged to three different tribes and spoke as many languages; the majority, however, knew something of Chinanja, the lake language, of which I had also learned a little, so we soon understood one another. It is always a wise arrangement to have different tribes in a caravan, for in the event of a strike, and there are always strikes, there is less chance of concerted action. Each man carried on his head a portion of my purse—which in this region consists solely of cloth and beads; while one or two of the more dependable were honored with the transportation of the tent, collecting-boxes, provisions, and guns.

The road struck into a banana grove, then through a flat country fairly well wooded with a variety of trees, including many palms and a few baobabs. The native huts dotted over this rich flat are the best I have seen in Africa. The roofs are trimly thatched, and a rude carving adorns door-post and lintel. After seven miles the Rukuru is crossed—a fine stream rippling over the sand, with large flakes of mica tumbling about in the current, and sampling the rocks of the distant hills. The men laid down their loads, and sprawled about like crocodiles in the water as I waded across. A few yards off is a village, where a fire was quickly lit, and the entire population turned out to watch the white man nibble his lunch. The consumption at this meal being somewhat slight, and the *menu* strange to my audience, I saw that they regarded the white man's effort at nutrition with feelings of contempt. " The M'sungu eats nothing," whispered one, " he must die." The head man presently came asking beads; but, as I had none unpacked, two stray trinkets and a spoonful of salt more than satisfied him. On getting the salt he deftly twisted a leaf into a little bag, and after pouring all the salt into it, graciously held out his hand to a troop of small boys who crowded round, and received one lick each of his empty palm. Salt is perhaps the greatest luxury and the greatest rarity the north-end African can have, and the avidity with which these young rascals received their homœo-pathic allowance proved the instinctiveness of the want. I have often offered native boys the choice between a pinch of salt and a knot of sugar, and they never failed to choose the first. For return-present the chief made over to me two large gourds filled with curds, of which, of course, I pretended to drink deeply before passing it on to the men.

Three miles of the same country, with tall bean-plants about, castor oil, and maize, but no villages in sight. Bananas unusually fine, and Borassus every-where. At the tent or eleventh mile we reached the fringe of hills bordering the higher lands, and, taking advantage of a passage about half a mile wide which has been cut by the river, penetrated the first barrier —a low rounded hill of conglomerate, fine in texture, and of a dark-red-color. Flanking this for two miles, we entered a broad oval expansion among the hills, the site apparently of a former lake. Winding along with the river for a mile or two more, and passing through a narrow and romantic glen, we emerged in a second valley, and camped for the night on the banks of the stream. On the opposite side stood a few native huts, and the occupants, after much re-connoitring, were induced to exchange some *ufa* and sweet potatoes for a little cloth.

1st October.—Moolu peered into my tent with the streak of dawn to announce a catastrophe. Four of the men had run away during the night. All was going so well yesterday that I flattered myself I was to be spared this traditional experience—the most exasperating of all the traveller's woes, for the whole march must be delayed until fresh recruits are enlisted to carry the deserters' loads. The delinquents were all Bandawé men. They had no complaint. They stole

nothing. It was a simple case of want of pluck. They
were going into a strange land. The rainy season
was coming on. Their loads were full-weight. So
they got homesick and ran. I had three more Bandawé men in the caravan, and, knowing well that the
moment they heard the news they would go and do
likewise, I ordered them to be told what had happened and then sent to my tent. In a few moments
they appeared ; but what to say to them ? Their
dialect was quite strange to me, and yet I felt I must
impress them somehow. Like the judge putting on
the black cap, I drew my revolver from under my
pillow, and, laying it before me, proceeded to address
them. Beginning with a few general remarks on
the weather, I first briefly sketched the geology of
Africa, and then broke into an impassioned defence of
the British Constitution. The three miserable sinners
—they had done nothing in the world—quaked like
aspens. I then followed up my advantage by inton-
ing in a voice of awful solemnity, the enunciation of
the Forty-Seventh Proposition of Euclid, and then
threw my all into a blood-curdling *Quod erat demon-
strandum.* Scene two followed when I was alone ; I
turned on my pillow and wept for shame. It was a
prodigious piece of rascality, but I cannot imagine
anything else that would have done, and it succeeded
perfectly. These men were to the end the most
faithful I had. They felt thenceforth they owed me
their lives ; for, according to African custom, the
sins of their fellow-tribesmen should have been visited
upon them with the penalty of death.

Seyid and Moolu scoured the country at once for
more carriers, but met with blank refusals on every
side. Many natives passed the camp, but they
seemed in unusual haste, and something of local
importance was evidently going on. We were not
long in doubt as to its nature. It was war. The
Angoni were in force behind a neighboring hill, and
had already killed one man. This might have been

startling, but I treated it as a piece of gossip, until
suddenly a long string of armed and painted men
appeared in sight and rushed past me at the double.
They kept perfect step, running in single file, their
feet adorned with anklets of rude bells which jingled
in time and formed quite a martial accompaniment.
The center man held aloft a small red and white flag,
and each warrior carried a large shield and several
light barbed spears. The regiment was led by a
fantastic looking creature, who played a hideous
slogan on a short pan-pipe. This main body was
followed at intervals by groups of twos and threes
who had been hastily summoned from their work,
and I must say the whole turnout looked very like
business. The last of the warriors had scarcely
disappeared before another procession of a different
sort set in from the opposite direction. It consisted
of the women and children from the threatened
villages farther up the valley. It was a melting
sight. The poor creatures were of all ages and sizes,
from the tottering grandmother to the week old
infant. On their heads they carried a miscellaneous
collection of household gods, and even the little
children were burdened with a calabash, a grass-mat,
a couple of fowls, or a handful of sweet-potatoes.
Probably the entire effects of the villages were
represented in these loads. Amongst the fugitives
were a few goats and one or two calves, and a troop
of boys brought up the rear driving before them a
herd of cows. The poor creatures quickened their
pace as they passed my tent, and eyed me as furtively
as if I and my men had been a detachment from the
Angoni executing a flank movement. The hamlet
opposite our camp, across the river, which had glad-
dened us the night before with its twinkling fires, its
inhabitants sitting peacefully at their doors or fishing
in the stream, was already deserted—the men to fight,
the woman to flee for their lives they knew not
whither. This is a common chapter in African

history.   Except among the very largest tribes no
man can call his home his own for a month.

I was amazed at the way my men treated the affair.
They lounged about camp with the most perfect
indifference.   This was accounted for by my presence.
The mere presence of a white man is considered an
absolute guarantee of safety in remoter Africa.   It is
not his gun or his imposing retinue ; it is simply
himself.   He is not mortal, he is a spirit.   Had I not
been there, or had I shown the white feather, my
men would have stampeded for Nyassa in a body.
I had learned to understand the feeling so thoroughly
that the events of the morning gave me no concern
whatever, and I spent the day collecting in the usual
way.

It was impossible to go on and leave the loads ;
it was equally impossible to get carriers at hand.
So I despatched Seyid with a letter to the station
on the Lake requesting six or eight natives to be
sent from there.   This meant a delay of two or three
days at least, which, with the rains so near, was
serious for me.

Made a "fly" for the tent, collected, and read.
One only feels the heat when doing nothing.   As
the sun climbed to its zenith my men put up for
themselves the most enticing bowers.   They were
ingeniously made with interlacing grasses and canes,
and densely thatched with banana leaves.

Tried twice to bake bread, with Jingo and Moolu
as assistant cooks.   Both attempts dismal failures, so
I had to draw on the biscuit-tins.   I have plenty of
fowls, bought yesterday for beads.   Maraya down
with fever.   One of the carriers, Siamuka, who had
been left behind sick, straggled into camp, looking
very ill indeed.   Physicked him and gave him four
yards of cloth to wrap himself in.   Towards sunset
I began to get anxious for news of battle.   The
arrival of the armed band which had passed in the
morning soon gratified me.   There had been no

battle. There had been no Angoni. It was simply
a scare—one of those false alarms which people in
these unsettled circumstances are constantly liable to.
All evening the women and children were trooping
back to their homes; and next morning our friends
opposite were smoking their pipes at the doors again,
as if nothing had happened.

Tuesday, 2d October—After morning cocoa had
a walk with my hammer to examine the sections in
the valley. Back to a good breakfast, cooked with
all the art of Jingo, the real cook being at Karongas
with the flag of distress. Moolu ill. This is the
third man down with fever since we left the Lake.
Bought some ufa and beans. Dispensed needles, and
bent pins for fish-hooks, among the men. Held a
great washing with Jingo. Towards the afternoon
the reinforcements arrived from Karongas. The chief
was drunk, it appeared, when my messenger reached
him; but Mr. Munro at the Lake kindly sent me a
number of his own men.

Another of my carriers begged leave to dissolve
our partnership, and produced two youths whom
he had beguiled into taking his load. His plea was
that he was in bad odor at Mweni-wanda, and was
afraid to go on. My own impression is that he found
the load which he carried—on his head, like all
Africans—was spoiling the cut of his hair. Even
Africa has its exquisites, and this man was the swell
all over. By "all over," I mean, of course, all over
his head, for as his hair is his only clothing, except
the bark loin cloth of which the cut cannot well be
varied, he had poured out the whole of his great soul
upon his coiffure. At the best the African's hair is
about the length of a toy-shop poodle's; but vanity
can make even a fool creative, and out of this scanty
material and with extraordinary labor he had com-
piled a masterpiece. First, heavily greased with
ground-nut oil, it was made up into small-sized balls
like black-currants, and then divided into symmetrical

patterns, diamonds, circles, and parterres, designed with the skill of a landscape-gardener. To protect this work of art from nightly destruction, this gentleman always carried with him a pillow of special make. It was constructed of wood, and dangled conspicuously from his spear-head on the march. He sold it to me ultimately for a yard of calico—and he certainly would not sleep after the transaction till he had laid the foundations of another.

12th October.—Got under weight at early dawn. Much shirking and dodging among the men for light loads. Formerly sudden and suspicious fevers used to develop at this critical juncture—by a not unaccountable coincidence among the men with the heaviest loads; but my now well-known mixture, compounded of pepper, mustard, cold tea, citrate of magnesia, Epsom salts, anything else that might be handy, and a flavoring pinch of cinchona, has miraculously stayed the epidemic. But I forgive these merry fellows everything for wasting none of the morning coolness over toilet or breakfast. I need not say the African never washes in the morning; but, what is of more importance, he never eats. He rises suddenly from the ground where he has lain like a log all night, gives himself a shake, shoulders his load, and is off. Even at the mid-day halt he eats little; but, if he can get it, will regale himself with a draught of water and a smoke. This last is a perfunctory performance, and one pipe usually serves for a dozen men. Each takes a whiff or two from the great wooden bowl, then passes it to his neighbor, and the pipe seldom makes a second round.

I often wondered how the natives produced a light when camping by themselves, and at last resolved to test it. So when the usual appeal was made to me for " motu," I handed them my vesta-box with a single match in it. I generally struck the match for them, this being considered a very daring experiment, and I felt pretty sure they would

make a mess of their one chance. It turned out as
I anticipated, and when they handed back the empty
box, I looked as abstracted and unapproachable as
possible. After a little suspense, one of them slowly
drew from the sewn-up monkey skin, which served
for his courier-bag, a small piece of wood about
three inches long. With a spear-head he cut in it a
round hole the size of a threepenny-piece. Placing
his spear-blade flat on the ground to serve as a base,
he stretched over it a scrap of bark-cloth torn from
his girdle, and then pinned both down with the
perforated piece of wood, which a second native held
firmly in position. Next he selected from among
his arrows a slender stick of very hard wood, inserted
it vertically in the hole, and proceeded to twirl it
round with great velocity between his open palms.
In less than half a minute the tinder was smoking
sulkily, and after a few more twirls it was ready for
further treatment by vigorous blowing, when it broke
into active flame. The fire originates, of course, in
the small soft piece of wood, from which sparks fall
upon the more inflammable bark-cloth at the bottom
of the hole.

Our daily programme, on the march, was something like this. At the first streak of dawn my
tent was struck. There is no time for a meal, for
the cool early hour is too precious in the tropics to
waste over eating; but a hasty coffee while the loads
were packing kept up the tradition of breakfast. In
twenty minutes the men were marshalled, quarrels
about an extra pound weight adjusted, and the procession started. At the head of the column I usually
walked myself, partly to see the country better,
partly to look out for game, and partly, I suppose,
because there was no one else to do it. Close
behind me came my own special valet—a Makololo
—carrying my geological hammer, water-bottle, and
loaded rifle. The white man, as a rule, carries
nothing except himself and a revolver, and possibly

a double-awned umbrella, which, with a thick pith helmet, makes sunstrokes impossible. Next Jingo marched the cook, a plausible Mananja, who could cook little, except the version of where the missing victuals went to. After the cook came another gentleman's gentleman carrying a gun and the medicine chest, and after him the rank and file, with another gun-bearer looking out for deserters at the rear. From half-past five I usually trudged on till the sun made moving torture, about ten or eleven. When I was fortunate enough to find shade and water there was a long rest till three in the afternoon, and an anomalous meal, followed by a second march till sunset. The dreadful part of the day was the interval. Then observations were made, and speci-mens collected and arranged, each man having to fill a collecting-box before sunset. When this was over there was nothing else to do that it was not too hot to do. It was too hot to sleep, there was nothing to read, and no one to speak to; the nearest post-office was a thousand miles off, and the only amusement was to entertain the native chiefs, who used occasion-ally to come with their followers to stare at the white man. These interviews at first entertained one vastly, but the humbling performances I had to go through became most intolerable. Think of having to stand up before a gaping crowd of savages and gravely button your coat—they had never seen a coat; or, wonder of wonders, strike a match, or snap a revolver, or set fire to somebody's bark clothes with a burning-glass. Three or four times a day often I had to go through these miserable performances, and I have come home with a new sympathy for sword-swallow-ers, fire-eaters, the man with the iron jaw, and all that ilk.

The interview commenced usually with the approach of two or three terror-stricken slaves, sent by the chief as a preliminary to test whether or not the white man would eat them. Their presents, native grains of some kind, being accepted, they concluded I was at least partly vegetarian, and the great man with his courtiers, armed with long spears, would advance and kneel down in a circle. A little speech-ifying followed, and then my return presents were produced—two or three yards of twopence-halfpenny calico ; and if he was a very great chief an empty Liebig pot or an old jam tin was also presented with great ceremony. None of my instruments, I found, at all interested these people—they were quite beyond them ; and I soon found that in my whole outfit there were not half a dozen things which conveyed any meaning to them whatever. They did not know enough even to be amazed. The greatest wonder of all perhaps was the burning-glass. They had never seen glass before, and thought it was *mazi* or water, but why the *mazi* did not run over when I put it in my pocket passed all understanding. When the light focused on the dry grass and set it ablaze their terror knew no bounds. "He is a mighty spirit!" they cried, "and brings down fire from the sun." This single remark contains the key to the whole secret of a white man's influence and power over all uncivilized tribes. Why a white man, alone and unprotected, can wander among these savage people without any risk from murder or robbery is a mystery at home. But it is his moral power, his education, his civilization. To the African the white man is a supreme being. His commonest acts are miracles; his clothes, his guns, his cooking utensils are super-natural. Everywhere his word is law. He can prevent death and war if he but speak the word. And let a single European settle, with fifty square miles of heathen round him, and in a short time he will be their king, their lawgiver, and their judge. I asked my men one day the question point blank— "Why do you not kill me and take my guns and clothes and beads ? " "Oh," they replied, " we would never kill a spirit." Their veneration for the white man indeed is sometimes most affecting. When war is brewing, or pestilence, they kneel before him and pray to him to avert it ; and so much do they believe in his omnipotence that an unprincipled man by trading on it, by simply offering pins, or buttons or tacks, or pieces of paper, or anything English, as charms against death, could almost drain a country of its ivory—the only native wealth.

The real dangers to a traveller are of a simpler kind. Central Africa is the finest hunting country in the world. Here are the elephant, the buffalo, the lion, the leopard, the rhinoceros, the hippopotamus, the giraffe, the hyæna, the eland, the zebra, and endless species of small deer and antelope. Then the whole country is covered with traps to catch these animals—deep pits with a jagged stake rising up in the middle, the whole roofed over with turf and grass, so exactly like the forest bed that only the trained eye can detect their presence. I have found myself walking unconsciously on a narrow neck between two of these pits, when a couple of steps to either side would almost certainly have meant death. Snakes too, and especially the hideous and deadly puff adder, may turn up at any moment ; and in bathing, which one eagerly does at every pool, the sharpest lookout is scarcely a match for the diabolical craft of the crocodile.

13th October.—Walking through the forest to-day some distance ahead of my men, I suddenly came upon a rhinoceros. The creature—the rhino is solitary in his habits—was poking about the bush with its head down and did not see me, though not ten yards separated us. My only arms were a geological hammer and a revolver, so I had simply to lie down and watch him. Presently my gun-bearer crawled up, but unfortunately by this time the pachyderm had vanished, and was nowhere to be found. I broke my heart over it at the moment, though why in the world I

should have killed him I do not in the least know
now. In cold blood one resents Mr. Punch's typical
Englishman—" What a heavenly morning! let's go
and kill something!" but in the presence of temptation one feels the veritable savage.

We are now at an elevation of about four thousand
feet, and steadily nearing the equator, although the
climate gives little sign of it. It is a popular mistake
that the nearer one goes to the equator the temperature must necessarily increase. Were this so, Africa,
which is the most tropical continent in the world,
would also be the hottest; while the torrid zone, which
occupies so large a portion of it, would be almost insupportable to the European. On the contrary, the
nearer one goes to the equator in Africa it becomes
the cooler. The reasons for this are twofold—the
gradual elevation of the continent towards the interior, and the increased amount of aqueous vapor in
the air. Central Africa is from three to five thousand
feet above the level of the sea. Now for every three
hundred feet of ascent the thermometer falls one degree. It is immensely cooler, therefore, in the interior than at the coast; and the equatorial zone all over
the world possesses a climate in every way superior
to that of the borders of the temperate region. At
night, in Equatorial Africa, it is really cold, and one
seldom lies down in his tent with less than a couple
of blankets and a warm quilt. The heat of New
York is often greater than that of Central Africa; for
while in America a summer rarely passes without the
thermometer reaching three figures, in the hottest
month in Africa my thermometer never registered
more than two on a single occasion—the highest
actual point reached being 96°. Nowhere, indeed, in
Africa have I experienced anything like the heat of
a summer in Malta, or even of a stifling August in
Southern Germany or Italy. On the other hand, the
direct rays of the sun are necessarily more powerful
in Africa; but so long as one keeps in the shade—

and even a good umbrella suffices for this—there is
nothing in the climate to disturb one's peace of mind
or body. When one really feels the high temperature is when down with fever; or when fever, unknown to one, is coming on. Then, indeed, the heat
becomes maddening and insupportable ; nor has the
victim words to express his feelings towards the glittering ball, whose daily march across the burnished
and veilless zenith brings him untold agony.

15th to 22d October—This camp is so well situated
that I have spent the week in it. The programme
is the same every day. At dawn Jingo came to my
tent with early coffee. Went out with my gun for a
morning stroll, and returned in an hour for breakfast.
Thereafter I sorted the specimens captured the day
before, and hung up the fatter insects to dry in the sun.
Routing the ants from the boxes and provision stores
was also an important and vexatious item. Some
ants are so clever that they can break into everything,
and others so small that they will crawl into anything ;
and between the clever ones, and the small ones,
and the jam-loving ones, and the flour-eating ones
and the specimen-devouring ones, subsistence, not to
say science, is a serious problem. The only things
that have hitherto baffled them are the geological
specimens ; but I overhaul these regularly every
morning along with the rest, in terror of one day
finding some precocious creature browsing off my
granites. After these labors I repaired to a natural
bower in the dry bed of a shaded streamlet, where I
spent the entire day. Here, even at high noon, was
perfect coolness, and rest, and solitude unutterable.
I lay among birds and beasts and flowers and insects,
watching their ways, and trying to enter into their unknown lives. To watch uninterruptedly the same
few yards of universe unfold its complex history ;
to behold the hourly resurrection of new living things,
and miss no change or circumstance, even of its

minuter parts ; to look at all, especially the things
you have seen before, a hundred times, to do all with
patience and reverence—this is the only way to
study nature.

Towards the afternoon the men began to drop in
with their boxes of insects, each man having to collect
a certain number every camp-day. If sufficient were
not brought in the delinquent had to go back to the
bush for more. At five or six I went back to my tent
for dinner, and after an hour over the camp-fire turned
in for the night. The chattering of the men all round
the tent usually kept me awake for an hour or two.
Their merriest time is just after sunset, when the great
ufa-feast of the day takes place. The banter between
the fires is kept up till the small hours, and the chief
theme of conversation is always the white man himself—what the whit man did, and what the white
man said, and how the white man held his gun, and
everything else the white man thought, looked, willed,
wore, ate, or drank. My object in being there was an
insoluble riddle to them, and for what witchcraft I collected all the stones and insects was an unending
source of speculation.

That they entered to some extent into one at least
of these interests was proved that very night. I was
roused rather late by a deputation, who informed me
that they had just discovered a very uncommon object
crawling on a stick among the firewood. Going out
to the fire and stirring the embers into a blaze, I was
shown one of the most extraordinary insects it has
been my lot to look upon. Rather over two inches
in length, the creature lay prone upon a branch,
adroitly shamming death, after the manner of the
Mantidæ, to which it obviously belonged. The striking feature was a glittering coal-black spiral, with a
large central spot of the same color, painted on the
middle of the back; the whole resembling a gigantic
eye, staring out from the body, and presenting the
most vivid contrast to the lemon yellows and greens

of the rest of the insect. One naturally sought a
mimetic explanation of the singular marking, and I
at once recalled a large fringed lichen which covered
many of the surrounding trees, and of which this
whole insect was a most apt copy. That it was as rare
as it was eccentric was evident from the astonishment
of the natives, who declared that they had never
seen it before.

22d October.—Water has been scarce for some days,
and this morning our one pool was quite dried up,
so I struck camp. Marching northwest, over an
undulating forest country, we came to a small village,
near which was a running stream. The chief, an
amiable old gentleman, after an hour spent in suspicious prospecting, came to see the show, and pro-
pitiated its leading actor with a present of flour.
In return I gave him some cloth and an empty magnesia bottle to hold his snuff. The native snuff-mull
is a cylinder of wood profusely carved, and, in the
absence of a pocket, hangs tied round the neck with
a thong. Snuffing is universal hereabouts.

This is a hotter camp than the last, though the
elevation (4500 feet) is nearly the same. Paid the
men their fortnight's wage in cloth, and as I threw
in an extra fathom they held high revelry till far on
in the night.

24th October.—Buffalo fever still on. Sallied
forth early with Moolu, a large herd being reported
at hand. We struck the trail after a few miles, but
the buffaloes had moved away, passing up a steep
valley to the north and clearing a hill. I followed,
but saw no sign, and after one or two unsuccessful
starts gave it up, as the heat had become terrific.
Breakfasted off wild honey, which one of the natives
managed to lay hands on, and sent for the camp to
come up. Moolu went on with one native, T'Shaula
—he of the great spear and the black feathers.

They returned about two o'clock announcing that they had dropped two bull buffaloes, but not being mortally wounded the quarry had made off. Late in the afternoon two of my men rushed in saying that one of the wounded buffaloes had attacked two of their number, one severely, and that assistance was wanted to carry them back. It seems that five of the men, on hearing Moolu's report about the wounded buffaloes, and tempted by the thought of fresh meat, set off without permission to try to secure them. It was a foolhardy freak, as they had only a spear with them, and a wounded buffalo bull is the most dangerous animal in Africa. It charges blindly at anything, and even after receiving its mortal wound has been known to kill its assailant. The would-be hunters soon overtook one of the creatures, a huge bull, lying in a hollow, and apparently *in articulo mortis*. They calmly walked up to it—the maddest thing in the world—when the brute suddenly roused itself and charged headlong. They ran for their lives one was overtaken and trampled down in a moment; the second was caught up a few yards farther on and literally impaled on the animal's horns. The first hobbled into camp little the worse, but the latter was brought in half dead. He had two frightful wounds, the less serious on the back behind the shoulder-blade, the other a yawning gash just under the ribs. I fortunately had a little lint and dressed his wounds as well as I could, but I thought he would die in my hands. He was quite delirious, and I ordered a watch all night in case the bleeding should break out afresh. His nurses unhappily could not take in the philosophy of this, and I had to turn out every hour to see that they were not asleep. The native's conception of pain is that it is the work of an evil spirit, and the approved treatment consists in blowing upon the wound and suspending a wooden charm from the patient's neck to exorcise it. All this was duly done now, and the blowing was repeated at frequent intervals through the night.

25th October. —Kacquia conscious, and suffering much. It is impossible to go on, so the men have rigged up a bower for me on the banks of a stream near the camp. Read, wrote, physicked right and left, and received the Chief of Something-or-other. Bribed some of his retinue to search the district for indiarubber, and bring specimens of the trees. After many hours, absence they brought me back two freshly-made balls, but neglected to bring a branch, which was what I promised to pay them for. From their description I gather the tree is the Landolphia vine. The method of securing the rubber is to make incisions in the stem and smear the exuding milky juice over their arms and necks. After it has dried a little they scrape it off and roll it up into balls.

An instance of what the native will do for a scrap of meat. Near camp this morning Moolu pointed out to me a gray lump on the top of a very high tree, which he assured me was an animal. It was a kind of lemur, and very good to eat. I had only my Winchester with me, and the ball ripped up the animal, which fell at once, but leaving an ounce or two of viscera on the branch. One of the men, Makata, coming up at the sound of the shot, perceived that the animal was not all there—it had been literally " cleaned"—immediately started to climb the tree for the remainder. It was a naked stem for a considerable height and thicker than himself, but he attacked it at once native fashion, *i.e*, by *walking* up the trunk, his clasped hands grasping the trunk on the opposite side from his doubled-up body, and literally walking upward on his soles. He soon came down with the precious mess, and in a few minutes it was cooked and eaten.

To-night I thought my hour was come. Our camp was right in the forest; it was pitch dark; and I was sitting late over the smouldering fire with the wounded man. Suddenly a terrific yell rang out from the forest, and a native rushed straight at me

brandishing his spear and whooping at the pitch of his
voice. Sure that it was an attack, I darted towards
the tent for my rifle, and in a second every man in the
camp was huddling in it likewise. Some dashed in
headlong by the door, others under the canvas, until
there was not room to crawl among their bodies.
Then followed—nothing. First an awful silence,
then a whispering, then a mighty laughter, and then
the whole party sneaked out of the fort and yelled
with merriment. One of my own men had crept out
a few yards for firewood; he had seen a leopard, and
lost control of himself—that was all. It was hard to
say who was most chaffed about it; but I confess I
did not realize before how simple a business it would
have been for any one who did not approve of the
white man to exterminate him and his caravan.

Sunday, 28th October.—My patient holding on; will
now probably pull through. As he has to be fed on
liquids, my own fowls have all gone in chicken soup.
Fowls are now very scarce, and my men, taking advantage of the high premium and urgent demand,
have gone long distances to get them. They will not
supply them to the invalid, but sell them to me to
give him. Wishing to teach them a lesson in phil-
anthropy, I declined to buy any more on these terms;
and after seeing me go three days dinnerless to give
Kacquia his chance of life they became ashamed of
themselves, and handed me all the fowls they had in
a present. This was a prodigious effort for a native,
and proves him capable of better things. The whole
camp had been watching this byplay for a day or two,
and the finish did good all round—more especially as
I gave a return present, after a judicious interval,
worth five times what had been given me.

Held the usual service in the evening—a piece of
very primitive Christianity. Moolu, who had learned
much from Dr. Laws, undertook the sermon, and dis-
coursed with great eloquence on the Tower of Babel.

The preceding Sunday he had waxed equally warm over the Rich Man and Lazarus; and his description of the Rich Man in terms of native ideas of wealth— " plenty of calico and plenty of beads "—was a thing to remember. " Mission-blacks," in Natal and at the Cape, are a byword among the unsympathetic; but I never saw Moolu do an inconsistent thing. He could neither read nor write; he knew only some dozen words of English; until seven years ago he had never seen a white man; but I could trust him with everything I had. He was not " pious "; he was neither bright nor clever; he was a commonplace black; but he did his duty and never told a lie. The first night of our camp, after all had gone to rest, I remember being roused by a low talking. I looked out of my tent; a flood of moonlight lit up the forest; and there, kneeling upon the ground, was a little group of natives, and Moolu in the centre conducting evening prayers. Every night afterwards this service was repeated, no matter how long the march was nor how tired the men. I make no comment. But this I will say—Moolu's life gave him the right to do it. Mission reports are often said to be valueless; they are less so than anti-mission reports. I believe in missions, for one thing, because I believe in Moolu.

But I need not go on with this itinerary. It is very much the same thing over again. For some time yet you must imagine the curious procession I have described wandering hither and thither among the wooded mountains and valleys of the table-land, and going through the same general programme. You might have seen its chief getting browner and browner in the tropical sun, his clothes getting raggeder and raggeder, his collecting-boxes becoming fuller and fuller, and his desire to get home again growing stronger and stronger. Then you might have seen the summer end and the tropical rains begin, and the whole country suddenly clothe itself with living green. And then, as the season advanced, you might

NEST OF THE WHITE ANT.

1, Male. 2, 4, 5, Neuters. 3, Gravid Female.

have seen him plodding back to the Lake, between the attacks of fever working his way down the Shiré and Zambesi, and so, after many days, greeting the new spring in England.

VI.

THE WHITE ANT.

A THEORY.

A FEW years ago, under the distinguished patronage of Mr. Darwin, the animal in vogue with scientific society was the worm. At present the fashionable animal is the ant. I am sorry, therefore, to have to begin by confessing that the insect whose praises I propose to sing, although bearing the honored name, is not entitled to consideration on account of its fashionable connections, since the white ant, as an ant, is an impostor. It is, in fact, not an ant at all, but belongs to a much humbler family—that of the *Termitidœ*—and so far from ever having been the vogue, this clever but artful creature is hated and despised by all civilized peoples. Nevertheless, if I mistake not, there is neither among the true ants, nor among the worms, an insect which plays a more wonderful or important part in nature.

Fully to appreciate the beauty of this function, a glance at an apparently distant aspect of nature will be necessary as a preliminary.

When we watch the farmer at work, and think how he has to plough, harrow, manure, and humor the soil before even one good crop can be coaxed out of it, we are apt to wonder how nature manages to secure her crops and yet dispense with all these accessories. The world is one vast garden, bringing forth crops of the most luxuriant and varied kind century after century, and millennium after millennium. Yet the face of nature is nowhere furrowed by the plough, no harrow disintegrates the clods, no lime and phosphates are strewn upon its fields, no visible tillage of the soil improves the work on the great world's farm.

Now, in reality, there cannot be crops, or successions of crops, without the most thorough agriculture ; and when we look more closely into nature we discover a system of husbandry of the most surprising kind. Nature does all things unobtrusively ; and it is only now that we are beginning to see the magnitude of these secret agricultural operations by which she does already all that man would wish to imitate, and to which his most scientific methods are but clumsy approximations.

In this great system of natural husbandry nature uses agencies, implements, and tools of many kinds. There is the disintegrating frost, that great natural harrow, which bursts asunder the clods by the expansion during freezing of the moisture imprisoned in their pores. There is the communistic wind which scatters broadcast over the fields the finer soil in clouds of summer dust. There is the rain which washes the humus into the hollows, and scrapes bare the rocks for further denudation. There is the air which, with its carbonic acid and oxygen, dissolves and decomposes the stubborn hills, and manufactures out of them the softest soils of the valley. And there are the humic acids, generated through decay, which filter through the ground and manure and enrich the new-made soils.

But this is not all, nor is this enough ; to prepare a surface film, however rich, and to manure the soil beneath, will secure one crop, but not a succession of crops. There must be a mixture and transference of these layers, and a continued mixture and transference, kept up from age to age. The lower layer of soil, exhausted with bringing forth, must be trans-

ferred to the top for change of air, and there it must lie
for a long time, increasing its substance, and recruit-
ing its strength among the invigorating elements.
The upper film, restored, disintegrated, saturated with
fertility and strength, must next be slowly lowered
down again to where the rootlets are lying in wait for
it, deep in the under soil.

Now how is this last change brought about? Man
turns up the crust with the plough, throwing up the
exhausted earth, down the refreshed soil, with infinite
toil and patience. And nature does it by natural
ploughmen who, with equal industry, are busy all
over the world reversing the earth's crust, turning it
over and over from year to year, only much more
slowly and much more thoroughly, spadeful by spadeful, foot by foot, and even grain by grain. Before
Adam delved the Garden of Eden these natural agri-
culturists were at work, millions and millions of them
in every part of the globe, at different seasons and in
different ways, tilling the world's fields.

According to Mr. Darwin, the animal which per-
forms this most important function in nature is the
earthworm. The marvellous series of observations
by which the great naturalist substantiated his conclusion are too well known for repetition. Mr.
Darwin calculates that on every acre of land in England more than ten tons of dry earth are passed
through the bodies of worms and brought to the
surface every year; and he assures us that the whole
soil of the country must pass and repass through
their bodies every few years. Some of this earth is
brought up from a considerable depth beneath the
soil, for, in order to make its subterranean burrow,
the animal is compelled to swallow a certain quantity of earth. It eats its way, in fact, to the surface,
and there voids the material in a little heap. Although the proper diet of worms is decaying vegetable matter, dragged down from the surface in the
form of leaves and tissues of plants, there are many

occasions on which this source of aliment fails, and
the animal has then to nourish itself by swallowing
quantities of earth, for the sake of the organic sub-
stances it contains. In this way the worm has a
twofold inducement to throw up earth. First, to
dispose of the material excavated from its burrow ;
and, second, to obtain adequate nourishment in times
of famine. "When we behold a wide, turf-covered
expanse," says Mr. Darwin, " we should remember
that its smoothness, on which so much of its beauty
depends, is mainly due to all the inequalities having
been slowly levelled by worms. It is a marvellous
reflection that the whole of the superficial mould
over any such expanse has passed, and will again
pass, every few years, through the bodies of worms.
The plough is one of the most ancient and most valuable of man's inventions ; but long before he existed
the land was, in fact, regularly ploughed by earth-
worms. It may be doubted whether there are many
other animals which have played so important a part
in the history of the world as have these lowly organized creatures."*

Now, without denying the very important contri-
bution of the earthworm in this respect, a truth sufficiently endorsed by the fact that the most circum-
stantial of naturalists has devoted a whole book to
this one animal, I would humbly bring forward another claimant to the honor of being, along with the
worm, the agriculturist of nature. While admitting
to the fullest extent the influence of worms in countries which enjoy a temperate and humid climate, it
can scarcely be allowed that the same influence is
exerted, or can possibly be exerted, in tropical lands.
No man was less in danger of taking a provincial
view of nature than Mr. Darwin, and in discussing
the earthworm he has certainly collected evidence
from different parts of the globe. He refers, al-

Vegetable Mould and Earth Worms, p. 313.

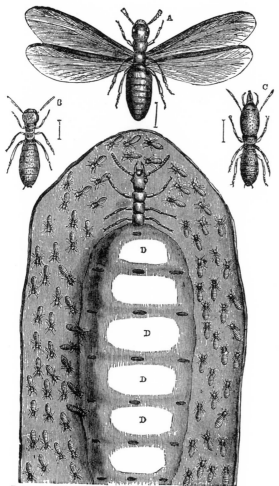

A, Male. B, Worker. C, Soldier. D, Fecundated Female of Termes bellicosus,
natural size, surrounded by ''Workers.''

though sparingly, and with less than his usual wealth of authorities, to worms being found in Iceland, in Madagascar, in the United States, Brazil, New South Wales, India, and Ceylon. But his facts, with regard especially to the influence, on the large scale, of the worm in warm countries, are few or wholly wanting. Africa, for instance, the most tropical country in the world, is not referred to at all ; and where the activities of worms in the tropics are described, the force of the fact is modified by the statement that these are only exerted during the limited number of weeks of the rainy season.

The fact is, for the greater portion of the year in the tropics the worm cannot operate at all. The soil, baked into a brick by the burning sun, absolutely refuses a passage to this soft and delicate animal. All the members of the earthworm tribe, it is true, are natural skewers, and though boring is their supreme function, the substance of these skewers is not hardened iron, and the pavement of a tropical forest is quite as intractable for nine months in the year as are the frost-bound fields to the farmer's ploughshare. During the brief period of the rainy season worms undoubtedly carry on their function in some of the moister tropical districts ; and in the sub-tropical regions of South America and India, worms, small and large, appear with the rains in endless numbers. But on the whole the tropics proper seem to be poorly supplied with worms. In Central Africa, though I looked for them often, I never saw a single worm. Even when the rainy season set in, the closest search failed to reveal any trace either of them or of their casts. Nevertheless, so wide is the distribution of this animal, that in the moister regions even of the equatorial belt one should certainly expect to find it. But the general fact remains. Whether we consider the comparative poorness of their development, or the limited period during which they can operate, the sustained performance of the agricultural function by worms, over large areas in tropical countries, is impossible.

Now as this agricultural function can never be dispensed with, it is more than probable that nature will have there commissioned some other animal to undertake the task. And there are several other animals to whom this difficult and laborious duty might be entrusted. There is the mole, for instance, with its wonderful spade-like feet, that natural navvy, who shovels the soil about so vigorously, at home ; but against the burnt crust of the tropics even this most determined of burrowers would surely turn the edge of his nails. The same remark applies to those curious little geologists the marmots and skipmunks, which one sees throwing up their tiny heaps of sand and gravel on the American prairies. And though the torrid zone boasts of a strong-limbed and almost steel-shod creature, the ant-bear, his ravages are limited to the destruction of the nests of ants ; and however much this somewhat scarce animal contributes to the result, we must look in another direction for the true tropical analogue of the worm.

The animal we are in search of, and which I venture to think equal to all the necessities of the case, is the termite or white ant. It is a small insect, with a bloated, yellowish-white body, and a somewhat large thorax, oblong-shaped, and colored a disagreeable oily brown. The flabby, tallow-like body makes this insect sufficiently repulsive, but it is for quite another reason that the white ant is the worst abused of all living vermin in warm countries. The termite lives almost exclusively upon wood ; and the moment a tree is cut or a log sawn for any economical purpose, this insect is upon its track. One may never see the insect, possibly, in the flesh, for it lives underground ; but its ravages confront one at every turn. You build your house, perhaps, and for a few months fancy you have pitched upon the one solitary site in the country where there are no

white ants. But one day suddenly the door-post
totters, and lintel and rafters come down together
with a crash. You look at a section of the wrecked
timbers, and discover that the whole inside is eaten
clean away. The apparently solid logs of which the
rest of the house is built are now mere cylinders of
bark, and through the thickest of them you could
push your little finger. Furniture, tables, chairs,
chests of drawers, everything made of wood, is in-
evitably attacked, and in a single night a strong
trunk is often riddled through and through, and
turned into matchwood. There is no limit, in fact,
to the depredation by these insects, and they will
eat books, or leather, or cloth, or anything; and in
many parts of Africa I believe if a man lay down to
sleep with a wooden leg it would be a heap of saw-
dust in the morning. So much feared is this insect
now, that no one in certain parts of India and Africa
ever attempts to travel with such a thing as a wooden
trunk. On the Tanganyika plateau I have camped
on ground which was as hard as adamant, and as
innocent of white ants apparently as the pavement
of St. Paul's, and wakened next morning to find a
stout wooden box almost gnawed to pieces. Leather
portmanteaus share the same fate, and the only sub-
stances which seem to defy the marauders are iron
and tin.

But what has this to do with earth or with agriculture? The most important point in the work of
the white ant remains to be noted. I have already
said that the white ant is never seen. Why he
should have such a repugnance to being looked at
is at first sight a mystery, seeing that he himself is
stone blind. But his coyness is really due to the
desire for self-protection, for the moment his juicy
body shows itself above ground there are a dozen
enemies waiting to devour it. And yet the white
ant can never procure any food until it comes above
ground. Nor will it meet the case for the insect to

come to the surface under the shadow of night.
Night in the tropics, so far as animal life is concerned, is as the day. It is the great feeding time,
the great fighting time, the carnival of the carnivores,
and of all beasts, birds, and insects of prey from the
least to the greatest. It is clear then that darkness
is no protection to the white ant; and yet without
coming out of the ground it cannot live. How does
it solve the difficulty? It takes the ground out
along with it. I have seen white ants working on
the top of a high tree, and yet they were underground. They took up some of the ground with
them to the tree-top; just as the Esquimaux heap
up snow, building it into the low tunnel-huts in
which they live, so the white ant collects earth, only
in this case not from the surface but from some
depth underneath the ground, and plaster it into
tunnelled ways. Occasionally these run along the
ground, but more often mount in endless ramifica-
tions to the top of trees, meandering along every
branch and twig, and here and there debouching into
large covered chambers which occupy half the girth
of the trunk. Millions of trees in some districts are
thus fantastically plastered over with tubes, galleries,
and chambers of earth, and many pounds weight of
subsoil must be brought up for the mining of even a
single tree. The building material is conveyed by
the insects up a central pipe with which all the
galleries communicate, and which at the downward
end connects with a series of subterranean passages
leading deep into the earth. The method of building
the tunnels and covered ways is as follows:—At the
foot of a tree the tiniest hole cautiously opens in the
ground close to the bark. A small head appears
with a grain of earth clasped in its jaws. Against
the tree-trunk this earth-grain is deposited, and the
head is withdrawn. Presently it reappears with
another grain of earth, this is laid beside the first,
rammed tight against it, and again the builder

THE MOUNDS OF THE WHITE ANT.

descends underground for more. The third grain is
not placed against the tree, but against the former
grain; a fourth, a fifth, and a sixth follow, and the
plan of the foundation begins to suggest itself as
soon as these are in position, The stones or grains
or pellets of earth are arranged in a semicircular
wall, the termite, now assisted by three or four
others, standing in the middle between the sheltering
wall and the tree, and working briskly with head and
mandible to strengthen the position. The wall in
fact forms a small moon-rampart, and as it grows
higher and higher it soon becomes evident that it is
going to grow from a low battlement into a long per-
pendicular tunnel running up the side of the tree.
The workers, safely ensconced inside, are now carrying up the structure with great rapidity, disappear-
ing in turn as soon as they have laid their stone and
rushing off to bring up another. The way in which
the building is done is extremely curious, and one
could watch the movement of these wonderful little
masons by the hour. Each stone as it is brought to
the top is first of all covered with mortar. Of course,
without this the whole tunnel would crumble into
dust before reaching the height of half an inch; but
the termite pours over the stone a moist sticky secre-
tion, turning the grain round and round with its
mandibles until the whole is covered with slime.
Then it places the stone with great care upon the
top of the wall, works it about vigorously for a
moment or two till it is well jammed into its place,
and then starts off instantly for another load.

Peering over the growing wall, one soon discovers
one, two, or more termites of a somewhat larger
build, considerably longer and with a very different
arrangement of the parts of the head, and especially
of the mandibles. These important-looking individuals saunter about the rampart in the most leisurely way, but yet with a certain air of business, as
if perhaps the one was the master of works and the

other the architect. But closer observation suggests that they are in no wise superintending operations, nor in any immediate way contributing to the structure, for they take not the slightest notice either of the workers or the works. They are posted there in fact as sentries, and there they stand, or promenade about, at the mouth of every tunnel, like sister Ann, to see if anybody is coming. Sometimes somebody does come in the shape of another ant—the real ant this time, not the defenceless *Neuropteron*, but some valiant and belted knight from the warlike *Formicidæ*. Singly, or in troops, this rapacious little insect, fearless in its chitinous coat of mail, charges down the tree-trunk, its antennæ waving defiance to the enemy, and its cruel mandibles thirsting for termite blood. The worker white ant is a poor defenceless creature, and blind and unarmed, would fall an immediate prey to these well-drilled banditti, who forage about in every tropical forest in unnumbered legion. But at the critical moment, like Goliath from the Philistines, the soldier termite advances to the fight. With a few sweeps of its scythe-like jaws it clears the ground, and while the attacking party is carrying off its dead, the builders, unconscious of the fray, quietly continue their work. To every hundred workers in a white ant colony, which numbers many thousands of individuals, there are perhaps two of these fighting men. The division of labor here is very wonderful, and the fact that besides these two specialized forms there are in every nest two other kinds of the same insect, the kings and queens, shows the remarkable height to which civilization in these communities has attained.

But where is this tunnel going to, and what object have the insects in view in ascending this lofty tree? Thirty feet from the ground, across innumerable forks, at the end of a long branch, are a few feet of dead wood. How the ants know it is there, how they know its sap has dried up, and that it is now fit for the termites' food, is a mystery. Possibly they do not know, and are only prospecting on the chance. The fact that they sometimes make straight for the decaying limb argues in these intances a kind of definite instinct ; but, on the other hand, the fact that in most cases the whole tree, in every branch and limb, is covered with termite tunnels, would show perhaps that they work most commonly on speculation, while the number of abandoned tunnels, ending on a sound branch in a *cul de sac*, proves how often they must suffer the usual disappointments of all such adventurers. The extent to which these insects carry on their tunnelling is quite incredible until one has seen it in nature with his own eyes. The tunnels are, perhaps, about the thickness of a small-sized gas-pipe, but there are junctions here and there of large dimensions, and occasionally patches of earthwork are found embracing nearly the whole trunk for some feet. The outside of these tunnels, which are never quite straight, but wander irregu-larly along stem and branch, resembles in texture a coarse sandpaper ; and the color, although this nat-urally varies with the soil, is usually a reddish brown. The quantity of earth and mud plastered over a single tree is often enormous ; and when one thinks that it is not only an isolated specimen here and there that is frescoed in this way, but often the whole of the trees of a forest, some idea will be formed of the magnitude of the operations of these insects and the extent of their influence upon the soil which they are thus ceaselessly transporting from underneath the ground.

In travelling through the great forest of the Rocky Mountains or of the Western States, the broken branches and fallen trunks strewing the ground breast-high with all sorts of decaying litter frequently make locomotion impossible. To attempt to ride through these western forests, with their meshwork of interlocked branches and decaying trunks, is often out of the question, and one has to dismount and drag his horse after him as if he were clambering through a woodyard. But in an African forest not a fallen branch is seen. One is struck at first at a certain clean look about the great forests of the interior, a novel and unaccountable cleanness, as if the forest-bed was carefully swept and dusted daily by unseen elves. And so, indeed, it is. Scavengers of a hundred kinds remove decaying animal matter —from the carcase of a fallen elephant to the broken wing of a gnat—eating it, or carrying it out of sight, and burying it on the deodorizing earth. And these countless millions of termites perform a similar function for the vegetable world, making away with all plants and trees, all stems, twigs, and tissues, the moment the finger of decay strikes the signal. Constantly in these woods one comes across what appear to be sticks and branches and bundles of faggots, but when closely examined they are seen to be mere casts in mud. From these hollow tubes, which preserve the original form of the branch down to the minutest knot or fork, the ligneous tissue is often entirely removed, while others are met with in all stages of demolition. Examine the section of an actual specimen, which is not yet completely destroyed, and from which the mode of attack may be easily seen. The insects start apparently from two centres. One company attacks the inner bark, which is the favorite morsel, leaving the coarse outer bark untouched, or more usually replacing it with grains of earth, atom by atom, as they eat it away. The inner bark is gnawed off likewise as they go along, but the woody tissue beneath is allowed to remain to form a protective sheath for the second company who begin work at the centre. This second contingent eats its way outward and onward, leaving a thin tube of the outer wood to the last, as props to the mine, till they have finished the main excavation. When a fallen trunk lying upon the ground is the object of attack,

NESTS OF WHITE ANTS.

the outer cylinder is frequently left quite intact, and
it is only when one tries to drag it off to his camp-
fire that he finds to his disgust that he is dealing
with a mere hollow tube a few lines in thickness filled
up with mud.

But the works above ground represent only a part
of the labors of these slow-moving but most indus-
trious of creatures. The arboreal tubes are only the
prolongation of a much more elaborate system of subterranean tunnels, which extend over large areas and
mine the earth sometimes to a depth of many feet or
even yards.

The material excavated from these underground
galleries and from the succession of domed chambers
—used as nurseries or granaries—to which they lead,
has to be thrown out upon the surface. And it is
from these materials that the huge ant-hills are reared,
which form so distinctive a feature of the African
landscape. These heaps and mounds are so conspicuous that they may be seen for miles, and so numerous are they and so useful as cover to the sportsman,
that without them in certain districts hunting would
be impossible. The first things, indeed, to strike the
traveller in entering the interior are the mounds of
the white ant, now dotting the plain in groups like a
small cemetery, now rising into mounds, singly or in
clusters, each thirty or forty feet in diameter and ten
or fifteen in height; or, again, standing out against
the sky like obelisks, their bare sides carved and
fluted into all sorts of fantastic shapes. In India
these ant-heaps seldom attain a height of more than
a couple of feet, but in Central Africa they form
veritable hills, and contain many tons of earth. The
brick houses of the Scotch mission-station on Lake
Nyassa have all been built out of a single ants' nest,
and the quarry from which the material has been
derived forms a pit beside the settlement some dozen
feet in depth. A supply of bricks, as large again,
could probably still be taken from this convenient

depôt; and the missionaries on Lake Tanganyika and onwards to Victoria Nyanza have been similarly indebted to the labors of the termites. In South Africa the Zulus and Kaffirs pave all their huts with white-ant earth; and during the Boer war our troops in Praetoria, by scooping out the interior from the smaller beehive-shaped ant-heaps, and covering the top with clay, constantly used them as ovens. These ant-heaps may be said to abound over the whole interior of Africa, and there are several distinct species. The most peculiar as well as the most ornate, is a small variety from one to two feet in height, which occurs in myriads along the shores of Lake Tanganyika. It is built in symmetrical tiers, and resembles a pile of small rounded hats, one above another, the rims depending like eaves, and sheltering the body of the hill from rain. To estimate the amount of earth per acre raised from the water-line of the subsoil by white ants would not in some districts be an impossible task; and it would be found, probably, that the quantity at least equalled that manipulated annually in temperate regions by the earthworm.

These mounds, however, are more than mere waste-heaps. Like the corresponding region underground, they are built into a meshwork of tunnels, galleries, and chambers, where the social interests of the community are attended to. The most spacious of these chambers, usually far underground, is very properly allocated to the head of the society, the queen. The queen-termite is a very rare insect, and as there are seldom more than one, or at most two, to a colony, and as the royal apartments are hidden far in the earth, few persons have ever seen a queen, and indeed most, if they did happen to come across it, from its very singular appearance, would refuse to believe that it had any connection with white ants. It possesses, indeed, the true termite head, but there the resemblance to the other members of the family stops,

for the size of the head bears about the same propor-
tion to the rest of the body as does the tuft on his
Glengarry bonnet to a six-foot Highlander. The
phenomenal corpulence of the royal body in the case
of the queen-termite is possibly due in part to want
of exercise, for once seated upon her throne she never
stirs to the end of her days. She lies there, a large,
loathsome, cylindrical package, two or three inches
long, in shape like a sausage, and as white as a bol-
ster. Her one duty in life is to lay eggs, and it must
be confessed she discharges her function with complete success, for in a single day her progeny often
amounts to many thousands, and for months this
enormous fecundity never slackens. The body in-
creases slowly in size, and through the transparent
skin the long folded ovary may be seen, with the
eggs, impelled by a peristaltic motion, passing onward
for delivery to the workers who are waiting to carry
them to the nurseries where they are hatched. Assid-
uous attention, meantime, is paid to the queen by
other workers, who feed her diligently, with much
self-denial stuffing her with morsel after morsel from
their own jaws. A guard of honor in the shape of a
few of the larger soldier-ants is also in attendance as
a last and almost unnecessary precaution. In addition, finally, to the soldiers, workers, and queen, the
royal chamber has also one other inmate—the king.
He is a very ordinary-looking insect, about the same
size as the soldiers, but the arrangement of the parts
of the head and body is widely different, and like the
queen he is furnished with eyes.

Let me now attempt to show the way in which
the work of the termites bears upon the natural
agriculture and geology of the tropics. Looking at
the question from the large point of view, the general
fact to be noted is, that the soil of the tropics is in
a state of perpetual motion. Instead of an upper
crust, moistened to a paste by the autumn rains, and
then baked hard as adamant in the sun ; and an under

soil hermetically sealed from the air and light, and inaccessible to all the natural manures derived from the decomposition of organic matters—these two layers being eternally fixed in their relations to one another—we have a slow and continued transference of the layers always taking place. Not only to cover their depredations, but to dispose of the earth excavated from the underground galleries, the termites are constantly transporting the deeper and exhausted soils to the surface. Thus there is, so to speak, a constant circulation of earth in the tropics, a ploughing and harrowing, not furrow by furrow and clod by clod, but pellet by pellet and grain by grain.

Some idea of the extent to which the underlying earth of the tropical forests is thus brought to the surface will have been gathered from the facts already described; but no one who has not seen it with his own eyes can appreciate the gigantic magnitude of the process. Occasionally one sees a whole trunk or branch, and sometimes almost an entire tree, so swathed in red mud that the bark is almost completely concealed, the tree looking as if it had been taken out bodily and dipped in some crystallizing solution. It is not only one tree here and there that exhibits the work of the white ant, but in many places the whole forest is so colored with dull red tunnels and patches as to give a distinct tone to the landscape—an effect which, at a little distance, reminds one of the *abend-roth* in a pine forest among the Alps. Some regions are naturally more favorable than others to the operations of the termites; and to those who have only seen them at work in India or in the lower districts of Africa this statement may seem an exaggeration. But on one range of forest-clad hills on the great plateau between Lake Nyassa and Tanganyika I have walked for miles through trees, every one of which, without exception, was ramified, more or less, with tunnels. The eleva-

tion of this locality was about 5000 feet above the sea
and the distance from the equator some 9° ; but nowhere else have I seen a spot where the termites were
so completely masters of the situation as here.   If it is
the case that in these, the most elevated regions of
Central Africa, the termite colonies attain their max-
imum development, the fact is of much interest in
connection with the geological and agricultural
function which they seem to serve ; for it is here precisely, before the rivers have gathered volume, that
alluvium is most wanting ; it is here that the tiny
headwaters of these same rivers collect the earth for
subsequent distribution over the distant plains and
coasts ; and though the white ant may itself have no
power, in the first instance, of creating soil, as a
denuding and transporting agent, its ministry can
scarcely be exaggerated.   If this is its function in
the economy of nature, it is certainly clear that the
insect to which this task is assigned is planted where,
of all places, it can most effectively fulfil the end.

The direct relation of the termites' work to
denudation will still further appear if we try to
imagine the effect upon the accumulations of earth
pellets and grains of an ordinary rainy season.   For
two or three months in the tropics, though intermittently, the rains lash the forests and soils with a fury
such as we, fortunately, have little idea of.   And
though the earthworks, and especially the larger
ant-hills, have marvellous resisting properties, they
are not invulnerable, and must ultimately succumb
to denuding agents.   The tunnels, being only required
for a temporary purpose, are made substantial enough
only to last the occasion.   And in spite of the
natural glue which cements the pellets of earth
together, the structure, as a whole, after a little
exposure, becomes extremely friable, and crumbles
to pieces at a touch.   When the earth-tubes crumble
into dust in the summer season the débris is scattered
over the country by the wind, and this way tends

to increase and refresh the soil. During the rains,
again, it is washed into the rivulets and borne away
to fertilize with new alluvium the distant valleys, or
carried downward to the ocean, where, along the
coast line, it "sows the dust of continents to be."
Herodotus, with equal poetic and scientific truth,
describes Egypt as "the gift of the Nile." Possibly
had he lived to-day he might have carried his vision
farther back still, and referred some of it to the
labors of the humble termites in the forest slopes
about Victoria Nyanza.

VII.

MIMICRY.

THE WAYS OF AFRICAN INSECTS.

MIMICRY is imposture in nature. Carlyle in his
blackest visions of "shams and humbugs" among
human kind never saw anything so finished in hypoc-
risy as the naturalist now finds in every tropical
forest. There are to be seen creatures, not singly,
but in tens of thousands, whose very appearance,
down to the minutest spot and wrinkle, is an affront
to truth, whose every attitude is a *pose* for a purpose,
and whose whole life is a sustained lie. Before these
masterpieces of deception the most ingenious of human
impositions are vulgar and transparent. Fraud is
not only the great rule of life in a tropical forest,
but the one condition of it.

Although the extraordinary phenomena of mimicry
are now pretty generally known to science, few workers have yet had the opportunity of studying them
in nature. But no study in natural history depends
more upon observation in the field; for while in the
case of a few mimetic forms—the *Heliconidæ*, for

example—the imitated form is also an insect, and the two specimens may be laid side by side in the cabinet at home, the great majority of mimetic insects are imitations of objects in the environment which cannot be brought into comparison with them in the drawers of a museum. Besides this, it is not only the form but the behavior of the mimetic insect, its whole habit and habitat, that have to be considered; so that mere museum contributions to mimicry are almost useless without the amplest supplement from the field naturalist. I make no further apology, therefore, for transcribing here a few notes bearing upon this subject from journals written during a recent survey of a region in the heart of Africa—the Nyassa-Tanganyika plateau—which has not yet been described or visited by any naturalist.

The preliminaries of the subject can be mastered in a moment even by the uninitiated, and I may therefore begin with a short preface on animal coloring in general. Mimicry depends on resemblances between an animal and some other object in its environment of which it is a practical gain to the creature to be a more or less accurate copy. The resemblance may be to any object, animate or inanimate. It may be restricted to color, or it may extend to form, and even to habit; but of these the first is by far the most imporant.

Apart from sexual selection, color in animals mainly serves two functions. It is either " protective" or " warning." The object of the first is to render the animal inconspicuous, the object of the second is the opposite—to make it conspicuous. Why it should be an object with some animals to be palpably exposed will be apparent from the following familiar instance of " warning" coloration. There are two great families of butterflies, the *Danaidœ* and *Acraiedœ*, which are inedible owing to the presence in their bodies of acrid and unwholesome juices. Now to swallow one of these creatures—and birds,

monkeys, lizards, and spiders are very fond of butterflies—would be gratuitous. It would be disappointing to the eater, who would have to disgorge
his prey immediately, and it would be an unnecessary
sacrifice of the subject of the experiment. These
butterflies, therefore, must have their disagreeable-
ness in some way advertised, and so they dress up
with exceptional eccentricity, distinguishing themselves by loud patterns and brilliant colorings, so
that the bird, the monkey, and the rest can take in
the situation at a glance. These animated danger-
signals float serenely about the forests with the utmost
coolness in the broadest daylight, leisureliness, defiance and self-complacency marking their every
movement, while their duskier brethren have to
hurry through the glades in terror of their lives. For
the same reason, well-armed or stinging insects are
always conspicuously ornamented with warning colors.
The expense of eating a wasp, for instance, is too
great to lead to a second investment in the same
insect, and wasps therefore have been rendered as
showy as possible so that they may be at once seen
and as carefully avoided. The same law applies to
bees, dragonflies, and other gaudy forms; and it
may be taken as a rule that all gayly-colored insects
belong to one or other of these two classes: that is,
that they are either bad eating or bad-stingers. Now
the remarkable fact is that all these brilliant and unwholesome creatures are closely imitated in outward
apparel by other creatures not themselves protected
by acrid juices, but which thus share the same immunity. That these are cases of mimicry is certain
from many considerations, not the least striking of
which is that frequently one of the sexes is protectively colored and not the other.

The brilliant coloring of poisonous snakes is
sometimes set down by naturalists to " warning," but
the details of coloring among reptiles have never been
thoroughly worked out. The difficulty suggests

itself that if the vivid yellows and oranges of some
snakes are meant to warn off dangerous animals,
the same conspicuousness would warn off the animals on which the venomous forms prey. Thus,
while *being* hunted, a showy skin might be of advantage to the snake ; in hunting it would be an
equal disadvantage. But when one watches on the
spot the manner in which snakes really do their
hunting, it becomes probable that the coloring,
vivid and peculiar as it is, in most cases is designed
simply to aid concealment. One of the most beautiful and ornate of all the tropical reptiles is the puff-
adder. This animal, the bite of which is certain
death, is from three to five feet long, and dispropor-
tionately thick, being in some parts almost as thick
as the lower part of the thigh. The whole body is
ornamented with strange devices in green, yellow,
and black, and lying in a museum its glittering coils
certainly form a most striking object. But in nature the puff-adder has a very different background.
It is essentially a forest animal, its true habitat being among the fallen leaves in the deep shade of the
trees by the banks of streams. Now in such a position, at the distance of a foot or two, its appearance
so exactly resembles the forest bed as to be almost
indistinguishable from it. I was once just throwing myself down under a tree to rest when, stoop-
ing to clear the spot, I noticed a peculiar pattern
among the leaves. I started back in horror to find
a puff-adder of the largest size, its thick back only
visible, and its fangs within a few inches of my face
as I stooped. It was lying concealed among fallen
leaves so like itself that, but for the exceptional
caution which in African travel becomes a habit, I
should certainly have sat down upon it, and to sit
down upon a puff-adder is to sit down for the last
time. I think this coloration in the puff-adder is
more than that of warning, and that this semi-som-
nolent attitude is not always the mere attitude of

repose. This reptile lay lengthwise, concealed all but a few inches, among the withered leaves. Now the peculiarity of the puff-adder is that it strikes *backward.* Lying on the ground, therefore, it commands as it were its whole rear, and the moment any part is touched, the head doubles backward with inconceivable swiftness, and the poison-fangs close upon their victim. The puff-adder in this way forms a sort of horrid trap set in the woods which may be altogether unperceived till it shuts with a sudden spring upon its prey.

But that the main function of coloring is protection may be decided from the simplest observation of animal life in any part of the world. Even among the larger animals, which one might suppose independent of subterfuge and whose appearance anywhere but in their native haunts suggests a very opposite theory, the harmony of color with environment is always more or less striking. When we look, for instance, at the coat of a zebra with its thunder-and-lightning pattern of black and white stripes, we should think such a conspicuous object designed to court rather than to elude attention. But the effect in nature is just the opposite. The black and white somehow take away the sense of a solid body altogether; the two colors seem to blend into the most inconspicuous gray, and at close quarters the effect is as of bars of light seen through the branches of shrubs. I have found myself in the forest gazing at what I supposed to be a solitary zebra, its presence betrayed by some motion due to my approach, and suddenly realized that I was surrounded by an entire herd which were all invisible until they moved. The motionlessness of wild game in the field when danger is near is well known; and every hunter is aware of the difficulty of seeing even the largest animals though they are just standing in front of him. The tiger, whose stripes are obviously meant to imitate the reeds of the jungle in which he lurks, is nowhere found in Africa; but its beautiful cousin, the leopard, abounds in these forests, and its spotted pelt probably conveys the same sense of indistinctness as in the case of the zebra. The hippopotamus seems to find the deep water of the rivers—where it spends the greater portion of its time—a sufficient protection; but the crocodile is marvellously concealed by its knotted mud-colored hide, and it is often quite impossible to tell at a distance whether the objects lying along the river banks are alligators or fallen logs.

But by far the most wonderful examples of protective adjustments are found where the further disguise of form is added to that of color, and to this only is the term mimicry strictly applicable. The pitch of intricate perfection to which mimicry has attained in an undisturbed and unglaciated country like Central Africa is so marvellous and incredible, that one almost hesitates to utter what his eyes have seen. Before going to Africa I was of course familiar with the accounts of mimetic insects to be found in the works of Bates, Belt, Wallace, and other naturalists; but no description prepares one in the least for the surprise which awaits him when first he encounters these species in nature. My introduction to them occurred on the borders of Lake Shirwa—one of the smaller and less known of the great African lakes—and I shall record the incident exactly as I find it in my notes. I had stopped one day among some tall dry grass to mark a reading of the aneroid, when one of my men suddenly shouted " Chirombo ! " " Chirombo " means an inedible beast of any kind, and I turned round to see where the animal was. The native pointed straight at myself. I could see nothing, but he approached, and pointing close to a wisp of hay which had fallen upon my coat, repeated " Chirombo ! " Believing that it must be some insect among the hay, I took it in my fingers, looked over it, and told him pointedly there was no " Chirombo "

there. He smiled, and pointing again to the hay, ex-
claimed "Moio!"—"It's alive!" The hay itself was
the Chirombo. I do not exaggerate when I say that
that wisp of hay was no more like an insect than my
aneroid barometer. I had mentally resolved never to
be taken in by any of these mimetic frauds; I was
incredulous enough to suspect that the descriptions
of Wallace and the others were somewhat highly colored; but I confess to have been completely stulti-
fied and beaten by the very first mimetic form I met.
It was one of that very remarkable family the *Phasmidæ*, but surely nowhere else in nature could there
be such another creature. Take two inches of dried
yellow grass-stalk, such as one might pluck to run
through the stem of a pipe; then take six other pieces
nearly as long and a quarter as thick; bend each in the
middle at any angle you like, stick them in three opposite pairs, and again at any angle you like, upon
the first grass stalk, and you have my Chirombo.
When you catch him, his limbs are twisted about at
every angle, as if the whole were made of one long
stalk of the most delicate grass, hinged in a dozen
places, and then gently crushed up into a dishevelled
heap. Having once assumed a position, by a wonderful instinct he never moves or varies one of his many
angles by half a degree. The way this insect keeps
up the delusion is indeed almost as wonderful as the
mimicry itself; you may turn him about and over
and over, but he is mere dried grass, and nothing will
induce him to acknowledge the animal kingdom by
the faintest suspicion of spontaneous movement. All
the members of this family have this power of shamming death; but how such emaciated and juiceless
skeletons should ever presume to be alive is the real
mystery. These Phasmidæ look more like ghosts
than living creatures, and so slim are they that, in
trying to kill them for the collecting-box, the strongest
squeeze between finger and thumb makes no more
impression upon them than it would upon fine steel

wire, and one has to half-guillotine them against some
hard substance before any little life they have is
sacrificed to science.

I examined after this many thousands of Phasmidæ,
Mantidæ, and other mimetic forms, and there is certainly in nature no more curious or interesting study.
These grass-stalk insects live exclusively among the
long grass which occurs in patches all over the forests,
and often reaches a height of eight or ten feet.
During three-fourths of the year it is dried by the
sun into a straw-yellow color, and all the insects are
painted to match. Although yellow is the ground
tone of these grasses, they are variegated, and
especially towards the latter half of the year, in two
ways. They are either tinged here and there with
red and brown, like the autumn colors at home, or
they are streaked and spotted with black mould or
other markings, painted by the finger of decay. All
these appearances are closely imitated by insects. To
complete the deception, some have the antennæ
developed to represent blades of grass, which are
often from one to two inches in length, and stick out
from the end of the body, one on either side, like
blades of grass at the end of a stalk. The favorite
attitude of these insects is to clasp a grass-stalk, as if
they were climbing a pole ; then the body is com-
pressed against the stem and held in position by the
two fore-limbs, which are extended in front so as to
form one long line with the body, and so mixed up
with the stalk as to be practically part of it. The
four other legs stand out anyhow in rigid spikes, like
forks from the grass, while the antennæ are erected
at the top, like blades coming off from a node, which
the button-like head so well resembles. When one of
these insects springs to a new stalk of grass it will at
once all but vanish before your eyes. It remains there
perfectly rigid, a component part of the grass itself,
its long legs crooked and branched exactly like dried
hay, the same in color, the same in fineness, and quite

defying detection. These blades, alike with limbs and body, are variously colored according to season and habitat. When the grasses are tinged with autumn tints they are the same; and the colors run through many shades, from the pure bright red, such as tips the fins of a perch, to the deeper claret colors or the tawny gold of port. But an even more singular fact remains to be noted. After the rainy season, when the new grasses spring up with their vivid color, these withered-grass insects seem all to disappear. Their color now would be no protection to them, and their places are taken by others colored as green as the new grass. Whether these are new insects or only the same in spring toilets I do not know; but I should think they are a different population altogether, the cycle of the former generation being, probably, complete with the end of summer.

Besides the insects which imitate grass, another large class imitate twigs, sticks, and the smaller branches of shrubs. The commonest of these is a walking twig, three or four inches long, covered with bark apparently, and spotted all over with mould like the genuine branch. The imitation of bark here is one of the most perfect delusions in nature; the delicate striation and the mould spots are reproduced exactly, while the segmentation of the body represents node-intervals with wonderful accuracy. On finding one of these insects I have often cut a small branch from an adjoining tree and laid the two side by side for comparison; and when both are partly concealed by the hands so as to show only the part of the insect's body which is free from limbs, it is impossible to tell the one from the other. The very joints of the legs in these forms are knobbed to represent nodes, and the characteristic attitudes of the insect are all such as to sustain the deception.

A still more elaborate set of forms are those which represent leaves. These belong mostly to the Mantis and Locust tribes, and they are found in all forms, sizes, and colors, mimicking foliage at every stage of growth, maturity and decay. Some have the leaf stamped on their broadened wing-cases in vivid green, with veins and midrib complete, and with curious expansions over the thorax and along all the limbs to imitate smaller leaves. I have again and again matched these forms in the forest, not only with the living leaf, but with crumpled, discolored, and shrivelled specimens, and indeed the imitations of the crumpled autumn-leaf are even more numerous and impressive than those of the living form. Lichens, mosses, and fungi are also constantly taken as models by insects, and there is probably nothing in the vegetal kingdom, no knot, wart, nut, mould, scale, bract, thorn, or bark, which has not its living counterpart in some animal form. Most of the moths, beetles, weevils, and especially the larval forms, are more or less protected mimetically ; and in fact almost the entire population of the tropics is guilty of personation in ways known or unknown. The lichen-mimicking insects even go the length of imitating holes, by means of mirror-like pools of black irregularly disposed on the back, or interrupting the otherwise dangerous symmetry of the fringed sides. The philosophy of these coal-black markings greatly puzzled me for a time. The first I saw was on a specimen of the singular and rare *Harpax ocellaria*, which had been thrown on the camp fire clinging to a lichen-covered log, and so well carried out was the illusion that even the natives were deceived till the culprit betrayed its quality by erecting its gauzy wings.

But it would be tedious to recount further the divisive ways of these arch-deceivers, and I shall only refer to another mimetic form, which for cool Pharisaism takes the palm from every creeping or flying thing. I first saw this *menteur à triple étage* on the Tanganyika plateau. I had lain for a whole week without stirring from one spot—a boulder in

the dried-up bed of a stream, for this is the only
way to find out what really goes on in nature. A
canopy of leaves arched overhead, the home of many
birds, and the granite boulders of the dry stream-
bed, and all along the banks, were marked with their
white droppings. One day I was startled to see one
of these droppings move. It was a mere white
splash upon the stone, and when I approached I saw
I must be mistaken; the thing was impossible; and
now it was perfectly motionless. But I certainly
saw it move, so I bent down and touched it. It was
an animal. Of course it was as dead as a stone the
moment I touched it, but one soon knows these
impostures, and I gave it a minute or two to become
alive—hastily sketching it meantime in case it
should vanish through the stone, for in that land of
wonders one really never knows what will happen
next. Here was a bird-dropping suddenly become
alive and moving over a rock; and now it was a
bird-dropping again; and yet, like Galileo, I protest
that it moved. It would not come to, and I almost
feared I might be mistaken after all, so I turned it
over on its other side. Now should any sceptic
persist that this was a bird-dropping I leave him to
account for a bird-dropping with six legs, a head,
and a segmented body. Righting the creature,
which showed no sign of life through all this ordeal,
I withdrew a few paces and watched developments.
It lay motionless on the stone, no legs, no head, no
feelers, nothing to be seen but a flat patch of white
—just such a patch as you could make on the stone
in a second with a piece of chalk. Presently it
stirred, and the spot slowly sidled across the boulder
until I caught the impostor and imprisoned him for
my cabinet. I saw in all about a dozen of these
insects after this. They are about half the size of a
fourpenny-piece, slightly more oval than round, and
as white as a snowflake. This whiteness is due to a
number of little tufts of delicate down growing out

from minute protuberances all over the back. It is
a fringe of similar tufts round the side that gives the
irregular margin so suggestive of a splash ; and the
under surface of the body has no protection at all.
The limbs are mere threads, and the motion of the
insect is slow and monotonous, with frequent pauses
to impress surrounding nature with its moribund
condition. Now, unless this insect with this color and
habit were protectively colored it simply would not
have a chance to exist. It lies fearlessly exposed on
the bare stones during the brightest hours of the
tropical day, a time when almost every other animal
is skulking out of sight. Lying upon all the stones
round about are the genuine droppings of birds ; and
when one sees the two together it is difficult to say
whether one is most struck with the originality of
the idea, or the extraordinary audacity with which
the *rôle* is carried out.*

It will be apparent from these brief notes that
mimicry is not merely an occasional or exceptional
phenomenon, but an integral part of the economy of
nature. It is not a chance relation between a few
objects, but a system so widely authorized that probably the whole animal kingdom is more or less
involved in it; a system, moreover, which, in the
hands of natural selection, must ever increase in
intricacy and beauty. It may also be taken for
granted that a scheme so widespread and so success-
ful is based upon some sound utilitarian principle.
That principle, I should say, was probably its *economy*.
Nature does everything as simply as possible, and
with the least expenditure of material. Now consider the enormous saving of muscle and nerve, of
instinct and energy, secured by making an animal's

* It is a considerable responsibility to be the sole witness to this
comedy—though I saw it repeated a dozen times subsequently—
but, fortunately for my veracity, I have since learned from Mr.
Kirby of the British Museum that there is an English beetle, the
Cionus Blattaria, the larval form of which "operates" in a precisely similar way.

lease of life to depend on passivity rather than activity. Instead of having to run away, the creature has simply to keep still; instead of having to fight, it has but to hide. No armor is needed, no powerful muscle, no expanse of wing. A few daubs of color, a little modelling of thorax and abdomen, a deft turn of antennæ and limb, and the thing is done.

At the first revelation of all these smart hypocrisies one is inclined to brand the whole system as cowardly and false. And, however much the creatures impress you by their cleverness, you never quite get over the feeling that there is something underhand about it; something questionable and morally unsound. The evolutionist, also, is apt to charge mimetic species in general with neglecting the harmonious development of their physical framework, and by a cheap and ignoble subterfuge evading the appointed struggle for life. But is it so? Are the æsthetic elements in nature so far below the mechanical? Are color and form, quietness and rest, so much less important than the specialization of single function or excellence in the arts of war? Is it nothing that, while in some animals the disguises tend to become more and more perfect, the faculties for penetrating them, in other animals, must continually increase in subtlety and power? And, after all, if the least must be said, is it not better to be a live dog than a dead lion?

VIII.

A GEOLOGICAL SKETCH.

FROM the work of the various explorers who have penetrated Africa, it is now certain that the interior of that Continent is occupied by a vast plateau from 4000 to 5000 feet above the level of the sea. In five separate regions—in the North-east, in Abyssinia, in the Masai country, on the Tanganyika plateau, and in the district inland from Benguela—this plateau attains a height of considerably over 5000 feet; while towards the coast, throughout their entire length, both east and west, it falls with great uniformity to a lower plateau, with an elevation of from 1000 to 2000 feet. This lower plateau is succeeded, also with much uniformity along both coast lines, by littoral and deltoid plains, with an average breadth from the sea of about 150 miles.

The section which I am about to describe, entering Africa at the Zambesi and penetrating inwards to the Tanganyika plateau, traverses each of these regions in turn—the coast-belt, the lower fringing table-land, the great general plateau of the country, and the third or highest elevation of the Tanganyika table-land. To deal thoroughly with so vast a region in the course of a single exploration is out of the question ; and I only indicate here a few of the rough results of what was no more than a brief and hasty reconnaissance.

The first and only geological feature to break the monotony of mangrove-swamp and low grass plain of the coast-belt is the débris of an ancient coral-reef, studded with sponges and other organisms. This reef is exposed on the Qua-qua River, a little above Mogurrumba, and about fifty miles from the sea. It is of small extent, at no great height above the present sea-level, and, taken alone, can only argue for a very inconsiderable elevation of the coast region. Some twenty miles farther inland, and still only a few yards above sea-level, an inconspicuous elevation appears, consisting of sedimentary rocks. This belt is traceable for some distance, both north and south, and a poor section may be found in the Zambesi River, a few miles above the grave of Mrs. Livingstone at Shupanga. The rocks in question, which are only visible when the Zambesi is very low, consist of a few thin beds of red and yellow sandstones, with intercalated marly sandstones and fine conglomerates. Sedimentary rocks, in somewhat similar relation, are found at least as far north as Mombassa, above Zanzibar, and as far south as the Cape; and it seems probable that the whole of the plateau of the interior is fringed by this narrow belt. No organic remains have been found in this series north of Natal, but the fossils of the Cape beds may shed some light on its horizon. Associated probably with these rocks are the great beds of coal which are known to exist some distance up the river in the neighborhood of Tette.

A short distance above the junction of the River Shiré with the Zambesi the first hills of the plateau begin almost abruptly. They occur in irregular isolated masses, mostly of the saddle-back order, and varying in height from 100 or 200 to 2000 feet. Those I examined consisted entirely of a very white quartzite—the only quartzite, I may say, I ever saw in East Central Africa. At the foot of the most prominent of those. hills—that of Morumballa—a hot-spring bubbles up, which Livingstone has already described in his "Zambesi." Hot-springs are not uncommon in other parts of the Continent, and several are to be found on the shores of Lake Nyassa. These are all of the simplest type, and although the temperature is high they leave no deposit anywhere to indicate their chemical character.

Two or three days' journey north and west of Morumballa, among the distant hills which border the valley of the Shiré, Livingstone marks a spot in his sketch-map where coal is to be found. After examining the neighborhood with some care, and cross-examining the native tribes, I conclude that Livingstone must, in this instance, have been either mistaken or misinformed. A black rock certainly occurs at the locality named, but after securing specimens of this as well as of all the dark-colored rocks in the vicinity, I found them to be, without exception, members of the igneous class. One very dark diorite was probably the rock which, on a distant view, had been mistaken for coal, for none of the natives along the whole length of the lower Shiré had ever heard of "a black rock which burned." Coal, however, as already mentioned, does certainly occur farther inland on the Zambesi; while, farther south, the Natal and Transvaal coalfields are now well known.

While speaking of coal I may best refer here to a small coal-bed associated with an apparently different series of rocks, and of special interest from its occurrence in the far interior of the country. On the western shore of Lake Nyassa, about 10° south latitude, coal was reported a few years ago by a solitary explorer, who penetrated that region prospecting for gold in the wake of Livingstone. The importance of such a discovery—a coal-seam on the borders of one of the great inland seas of Africa—cannot be over-estimated; and the late Mr. James Stewart, C.E., who has done such important work for the geography of Africa, made a special examination of the spot. From his report to the Royal Geographical Society I extract the following reference:—

"On the 29th we marched northwards along the coast, reaching, after three miles, the stream in which is the coal discovered by Mr. Rhodes. The coal lies in a clay bank, tilted up at an angle of 45°, dip west. It is laid bare over only some 30 feet, and is about 7 feet thick. It hardly looks as if it were in its original bed. The coal is broken and thrown about as if it had been brought down by a landslip, and traces of clay are found in the interstices. Yet the bed is compact, and full of good coal. I traced it along the hillside for some 200 yards, and found it cropping out on the surface here and there. It is 500 feet above the lake-level, and about a mile and a half from the shore. I lit a good fire with it, which burned up strongly. The coal softened and threw out gas bubbles, but gave no gas-jets. It caked slightly, but not so as to impede its burning."—*Proceedings*, vol. iii. No. 5, p. 264.

I examined this section pretty carefully, and fear I must differ slightly from Mr. Stewart in his geological and economical view of the formation. The 7-foot seam described by Stewart is certainly a deception, the seam being really composed of a series of thin beds of alternately carbonaceous and argillaceous matter, few of the layers of coal being more than an inch in thickness. With some of the most carefully selected specimens I lit a fire, but with disappointing results. Combustion was slow, and without flame. Although there were what can only be called *films* of really good coal here and there, the mineral, on the whole, seemed of inferior quality, and useless as a steam-coal. From the general indications of the locality I should judge that the coal existed only in limited quantity, while the position of the bed at the top of a rocky gorge renders the deposit all but inaccessible. On the whole, therefore, the Lake Nyassa coal, so far as opened up at present, can scarcely be regarded as having any great economical importance, although the geological interest of such a mineral in this region is considerable. Sections of the coal have already been prepared for the microscope, and Dr. Carruthers of the British Museum has identified the macrospores of Lycopodaceous plants, which are identical with similar organisms found in the coal-fields of England.

The Geology of the great African plateaux, so far as my section from the Lower Shiré to the Tanganyika plateau is any indication of their general structure, is of such simplicity that it may almost be dismissed in a sentence. The whole country from the Shiré river, a hundred miles above its junction with the Zambesi, embracing the lower and higher central plateaux, the whole Shiré Highlands from the river to the westward shores of Lake Shirwa, the three

hundred miles of rocky coast fringing the western
shore of Lake Nyassa, the plateau between Nyassa
and Tanganyika for at least half its length—with
one unimportant interruption—consists solely of granite and gneiss.   The character and texture of this
rock persist with remarkable uniformity throughout
this immense region.   The granite, an ordinary gray
granite, composed of white rarely pink orthoclase
felspar, the mica of the biotitic or magnesian variety,
rarely muscovite, and neither fine nor coarse in texture; the gneiss, the same rock foliated.   Of the relation of these gneissose and granitic rocks to one
another I was unable to discover any law.   Sometimes
the gneiss would persist over a large area, sometimes
the granite; while frequently the two would alternate
perplexingly within a limited area.   Mr. Joseph
Thomson's section, drawn inland from Zanzibar and
joining mine at the northern end of Lake Nyassa, and
thence onwards by a more easterly route towards
Tanganyika, reveals a somewhat similar petrograph-
ical structure; and, from scattered references in
the journals of other explorers, it is plain that this
gneisso-granitic formation occupies a very large area
in the interior of the African Continent.   Associated
minerals with these rocks, as far as a very general
survey indicated, were all but wholly wanting.   At
Zomba, on the Shiré Highlands, a little tourmaline
occurs, but of the precious metals I could find no
trace.   Veins of any kind are also rare; and even
pegmatite I encountered in only one instance.   In-
trusive dykes throughout the whole area were likewise absent except in a single district.   This district
lies towards the southern border of the Shiré Highlands, immediately where the plateau rises from the
river, and there the dykes occur pretty numerously.
They are seldom more than a few feet in breadth,
and consist of ordinary dolerite or basalt.   The black
rock on the Lower Shiré, already mentioned in connection with Livingstone's supposed discovery of coal,

may possibly be one of these dykes; but that there is any considerable development of igneous rocks in this immediate locality I should doubt. Farther up the Zambesi, however, coulées of basalt are met with at more than one place, conspicuously in the neighborhood of the Victoria Falls. The only distinct trace of volcanic action throughout my route appeared towards the extreme northern end of Lake Nyassa. One is warned beforehand by occasional specimens of pumice lying about the lake shore as one travels north; but it is not till the extreme end of the lake is reached that the source is discovered in the series of low volcanic cones which Thomson has already described in this locality. The development is apparently local, and the origin of the cones probably comparatively recent.

Apart from this local development of igneous rocks at the north end of Lake Nyassa, the only other break in the granitic series throughout the area traversed by my line of march occurs near the native village of Karonga, on Lake Nyassa. About a dozen miles from the north-western lake shore on the route to Tanganyika, after following the Rukuru river through a defile of granite rocks, I came, to my great surprise, upon a well-marked series of stratified beds. At a bend in the river a fine section is exposed. They lie throw against the granitic rocks, which here show signs of disturbance, and consist of thin beds of very fine light-gray sandstone, and blue and gray shales, with an occasional band of gray limestone. By camping at the spot for some days, and working patiently, I was rewarded with the discovery of fossils. This is, of course, the main interest of these beds,—for these are, I believe, the only fossils that have ever been found in Central Africa. The shale, naturally, yielded the most productive results, one layer especially being one mass of small *Lamellibranchiata.* Though so numerous, these fossils are confined to a single species of the *Tellinidae*, a family abundantly represented in tropical seas at the present time, and dating back as far as the Oolite. Vegetable remains are feebly represented by a few reeds and grasses. Fish-scales abound ; but I was only able, and that after much labor, to unearth two two or three imperfect specimens of the fishes themselves. These have been put into the accomplished hands of Dr. Traquair of Edinburgh, who has been kind enough to furnish the following account of them :—

EDINBURGH, 23d April, 1888.

DEAR PROFESSOR DRUMMOND—I have carefully examined the six specimens of fossil fish-remains from Central Africa, which you submitted to me, and though I certainly would have wished them to have been less fragmentary, I shall do my best to give an opinion upon them.

No. 1, the largest, is the hinder portion of a fish of moderate size, showing not only scales, but also the remains of the dorsal, anal, and caudal fins. The caudal is strongly heterocercal, and was probably deeply bifurcated, but the rays of the lower lobe are very badly preserved : only the posterior parts of the dorsal and anal are seen, nearly opposite each other, and composed of fine, closely placed, and closely articulated rays. The scales, displaced and jumbled up, are osseous, thick, and rhomboidal, with a strong blunt carina on the attached surface, while the exposed part of the external surface is covered with ganoine, and ornamented with rather sparsely scattered pits and punctures.

Belonging to the Order Ganoidei, this fish is with equal certainty referable to the family Palæoniscidæ, but its *genus* is more a matter of doubt owing to the fragmentary nature of the specimen. Judging from the form and thickness of the scales, I should be inclined to refer it to *Acrolepis*, were it not that the dorsal and anal fins seem so close to the tail, and so nearly opposite each other ; here, however, it may be remarked that the disturbed state of the scales affords room for the possibility that the original relations of the parts may not be perfectly preserved. I have, however, no doubt that, as a *species*, it is new; and as you have been the first to bring fossil fishes from those regions of Central Africa, you will perhaps allow me to name it *Acrolepis* (?) *Drummondi*.

No. 2 is a piece of cream-colored limestone, with numerous minute, scattered, rhombic, striated, ganoid scales, which I cannot venture to name, though I believe them to be palæoniscid. Associated with these is a small portion of the margin of a jaw, with numerous minute sharp conical teeth. But also lying among these minuter relics is a scale of a much larger size, and clearly belonging to another fish. It measures 1-4 inch in height by the same in breadth; its shape is rhomboidal, having an extensive anterior covered area, and a strong articular spine projecting from the upper margin. The free surface is brilliantly ganoid, and marked with furrows separating feeble ridges, which pass rather obliquely downwards and backwards across the scale, and terminate in eight sharp denticulations of the hinder margin. A little way off is the impression of the attached surface of a similar scale, and there are also two interspinous bones, probably belonging to the same fish.

This is probably also a palæoniscid scale, resembling in shape those of *Acrolepis*, but it is rather thinner than is usually the case in this genus. It has also considerable resemblance to some of those scales from the European Trias, named by Agassiz *Gyrolepis*. Though it may be rather venturesome to name a species from such slender material, nevertheless we may, provisionally at least, recognize the scale as *Acrolepis* (?) *Africanus*.

Nos. 3 and 4 are small pieces of the same limestone, covered with the minute striated palæoniscid scales referred to above.

No. 5 is a piece of gray micaceous shale, with scales of yet a fourth species of palæoniscid fish. One conspicuous scale unfortunately, like all the rest, seen only from the attached surface, is 1-4 inch in height by nearly 1-6 in breadth; it is tolerably rectangular in shape, having a well-developed articular spine and fossette. Part of the scale is broken away at the anterior margin, the impression brought into view showing that the covered area is narrow, and indicating that the free surface is striated with rather sharp ridges passing obliquely across the scale. The posterior margin is finely denticulated.

Though this scale is in my opinion specifically, and possibly generically, distinct from those previously named, the outer surface not being properly displayed renders it impossible to give a sufficient diagnosis.

No. 6 is a piece of the same shale, having the clavicle of a small palæoniscid fish, which it is, however, impossible to name.—I am, yours faithfully,

R. H. TRAQUAIR.

These fossiliferous beds seem to occupy a comparatively limited area, and have a very high dip in a south-easterly direction. At the spot where my observations were taken they did not extend over more than half a mile of country, but it is possible that the formation may persist for a long distance in other directions. Indeed, I traced it for some miles in the direction in which, some fifty or sixty miles off, lay the coal already described, and to which it may possibly be related.

With one or two general remarks upon surface geology and physical geography I bring this note to a close. First, regarding the Lakes Nyassa and

Shirwa,—there is distinct evidence, and especially in the case of the latter, that they have formerly occupied a considerably larger area than at present. Shirwa is an extremely shallow lake ; though the eastern and southern shores are mountainous, it is suggestive rather of an immense bog than of a deep inland sea. For many miles before reaching the shore there are signs that one is traversing the site of a former and larger Shirwa, which may possibly at one time have been actually connected with the lower extremity of Lake Nyassa. To substantiate this conclusion, however, will require more detailed examination of the Shiré Highlands than I was able to give. The peculiarity of Shirwa is that the water is brackish to the taste, while that of Nyassa and of the other Central African lakes, with the exception of Lake Leopold, is fresh. The shallowness of Shirwa, and the precariousness of its outlet through Lake Cheuta to the Lujenda, amply account for this difference ; for the narrow waters of Nyassa and Tanganyika are thoroughly drained and profoundly deep.

That Lake Nyassa is also slowly drying up is evident from the most superficial examination of its southern end. There it has already left behind a smaller lake—Lake Pomalombé—a considerable expanse of water, through which the Shiré passes a few miles after emerging from Lake Nyassa, but already so shallow that nowhere in the dry season does the depth exceed three fathoms. If the silting up of this lake continues for a few years it will render this sheet of water, which commands the entrance to Lake Nyassa, totally unnavigable, and thus close the magnificent water-highway at present open, with a portage of seventy miles, from the top of Lake Nyassa to the Indian Ocean at the mouth of the Zambesi.

Regarding the interesting question of the origin of Lake Nyassa and its great sister-lakes in the heart of Africa—the Victoria and Albert Nyanza

and Tanganyika—I do not presume to speak. No
follower of Ramsay in his theory of the glacial origin
of lakes could desire a more perfect example of a
rock-basin than that of Lake Nyassa. It is a gigantic
trough of granite and gneiss, three hundred miles in
length, nowhere over fifty miles in breadth, and
sixteen hundred feet above the level of the sea,
the mountains rising all around it, and sometimes
almost sheer above it, to a farther height of one,
two, and three thousand feet. The high Tanganyika plateau borders it on the northern shore, and
the greatest depth is precisely where the glacial
theory would demand, namely, towards the upper
portion of the lake. On the other hand, the physical
geology of the country in which these other lakes
are situated, as well as several features connected
with Lake Nyassa itself, lend no countenance to such
a view ; and probably the suggestion of Murchison
and other geologists is correct, that all these lakes,
colossal though they still are, are the remnants of a
much vaster expanse of water which once stretched
over Central Africa.

The only other point to which I need allude is the
subject of glaciation itself. And I refer to this
pointedly, because I have lately encountered allu-
sions, and in quarters entitling them to respect, to
the presence of glacial phenomena in the Central
Lake district of Africa. I confess that my observations have failed to confirm these suggestions. It
has been my lot to have had perhaps exceptional
opportunities of studying the phenomena of glaciation in Europe and Northern America, and I have
been unable to detect anywhere in the interior of
Africa a solitary indication of glacial action. In
Kaffirland, far to the south, there are features which
one would almost unhesitatingly refer to glaciation ;
but in East Central Africa not a vestige of boulder-
clay, nor moraine matter, nor striæ, nor glaciated
surface, nor outline, is anywhere traceable. One

would be curious to know to what extent the flora and fauna of the inland plateau confirm or contradict this negative evidence against the glaciation of this region.

Finally, the thing about the geology of Africa that strikes one as especially significant is that throughout this vast area, just opening up to science, there is nothing new—no unknown force at work ; no rock strange to the petrographer ; no pause in denudation ; no formation, texture, or structure to put the law of continuity to confusion. Rapid radiation, certainly, replaces the effects of frost in northern lands—and the enormous denudation due to this cause is a most striking feature of tropical geology. The labors of the worm, again, in transporting soil in temperate climates are undertaken by the termite ; but here, as elsewhere, every fresh investigation tends to establish more and more the oneness and simplicity of Nature.

<hr/>

IX.

A POLITICAL WARNING.

WHEN I reached the coast to embark for England after my wanderings in the interior, the Portuguese authorities at Quilimane presented me with various official documents, which I was told I must acknowledge with signatures and money before being permitted to leave Africa. Having already had to pay certain moneys to Portugal to get into this country, it was a shock to find that I had also to pay to get out; but, as no tax could be considered excessive that would facilitate one's leaving even the least of the Portuguese East African colonies, I cheerfully counted out the price of my release. Before completing the conveyance, however, my eye

fell on six words prominently endorsed on one of
the documents, which instantly tightened my purse-
strings. The words were, "TAX FOR RESIDING IN
THE INTERIOR "—so much. Now a day or two spent
in waiting for a steamer could scarcely be construed
into residence, nor could a strip of coast-line with
propriety be termed the interior, so I ventured to point
out the irrelevancy to the Portuguese official. Waiv-
ing the merely philological question of residence, he
went at once to the root of the matter by informing
me that the Portuguese definition of the word Interior differed materially from that of England. The
Interior, he said, comprised the whole of Africa inland
from the coast-province of Mozambique, and included,
among other and larger possessions, the trifling territories of the Upper Shiré Highlands, Lake Shirwa,
and Lake Nyassa. These last, he assured me, belonged to Portugal, and it became me, having therein
shared the protection of that ancient flag, to acknowledge the obligation to the extent of so many
hundred Reis.

Though not unprepared for this assumption, the
idea of enforcing it by demanding tribute was so
great a novelty that, before discharging my supposed
liabilities, I humbly asked information on the following points :—1. Did the region described really belong
to Portugal ? 2. When and where was this claim
recognized by England directly or indirectly ? 3.
Where in the Interior, as thus defined, was the Portuguese flag to be found ? And 4. What protection
had it ever given to me or to any other European ?
The replies to these queries being evasive, I took it
upon myself to correct the history, the geography,
and the politics of the throng of Government officials
who now joined the sederunt by the following statement of facts :—1. The region described did not
belong to Portugal. 2. Its sovereignty had never
been in any way acknowledged by England. 3. The
Portuguese flag was nowhere to be found there, and

never had been there. 4. Not one solitary Portuguese up to that time had ever even set foot in the
country—except one man who was brought in for a
few weeks under English auspices ; so that no protection had ever been given, or could possibly be
given, to me or to any one else. These statements
were received in silence, and after much running to
and fro among the officials the representative of John
Bull, instead of being dragged to prison, and his rifle
—his only real escort through Nyassa-land—poinded
to pay for his imaginary protection, found himself
bowed off the premises with a discharge in full of his
debt to Portugal, and the unpaid tax-paper still in
his pocket.

I recall this incident to introduce in all seriousness
the question interesting so many at the present
moment as to the title-deeds of Equatorial Africa.
Why Africa should not belong to the Africans I have
never quite been able to see, but since this Continent
is being rapidly partitioned out among the various
European States, it is well, even in the African interest, to inquire into the nature and validity of these
claims. The two political maps which will be found
at the end of this volume will enable those interested
to see the present situation at a glance, and I shall
only further emphasize one or two points of immediate practical importance.

The connection of Portugal with Africa is an old,
and—at least it was at first—an honorable one. The
voyages of the Portuguese were the first to enrich
geography with a knowledge of the African coasts,
and so early as 1497 they took possession of the
eastern shore by founding the colony of Mozambique.
This rule, however, though nominally extending
from Delagoa Bay to as far north as Cape Delgado,
was confined to two or three isolated points, and
nowhere, except on the Zambesi, affected more than
the mere fringe of land bordering the Indian Ocean.
On the Zambesi the Portuguese established stations

at Senna, Tette, and Zumbo, which were used, though on the most limited scale, as missionary and trading centres; but these are at present all but abandoned and in the last stages of decrepitude. The right of Portugal to the lower regions of the Zambesi, notwithstanding its entire failure to colonize in and govern the country, can never be disputed by any European Power, though the Landeens, or Zulus, who occupy the southern bank, not only refuse to acknowledge the claim, but exact an annual tribute from the Portuguese for their occupation of the district.

No one has ever attempted to define how far inland the Portuguese claim, founded on coast-possession, is to be considered good; but that it cannot include the regions north of the Zambesi—the Shiré Highlands and Lake Nyassa—is self-evident. These regions were discovered and explored by Livingstone. They have been occupied since his time exclusively by British subjects, and colonized exclusively with British capital. The claim of England, therefore— though nothing but a moral claim has ever been made—is founded on the double right of discovery and occupation; and if it were a question of treaty with the natives, it might possibly be found on private inquiry that a precaution so obvious had not been forgotten by those most nearly interested. On the other hand, no treaties exist with Portugal; there is not a single Portuguese in the country, and until the other day no Portuguese had even seen it. The Portuguese boundary-line has always stopped at the confluence with the Shiré of the river Ruo, and the political barrier erected there by Chipitula and the river Chiefs has been maintained so rigidly that no subject of Portugal was ever allowed to pass it from the south. Instead, therefore, of possessing the Shiré Highlands, that is the region of all others from which the Portuguese have been most carefully excluded.

The reason for this enforced exclusion is not far to seek. At first the Portuguese had too much to do in keeping their always precarious foothold on the banks of the Zambesi to think of the country that lay beyond; and when their eyes were at last turned towards it by the successes of the English, the detestation in which they were by this time held by the natives—the inevitable result of long years of tyranny and mismanagement—made it impossible for them to extend an influence which was known to be disastrous to every native right. Had the Portuguese done well by the piece of Africa of which they already assumed the stewardship, no one now would dispute their claim to as much of the country as they could wisely use. But when even the natives have had to rise and by force of arms prevent their expansion, it is impossible that they should be allowed to overflow into the Highland country—much less to claim it—now that England, by pacific colonization and missionary work, holds the key to the hearts and hands of its peoples. By every moral consideration the Portuguese have themselves forfeited the permission to trespass farther in Equatorial Africa. They have done nothing for the people since the day they set foot in it. They have never discouraged, but rather connived at, the slave-trade; Livingstone himself took the servant of the Governor of Tette red-handed at the head of a large slave-gang. They have been at perpetual feud with the native tribes. They have taught them to drink. Their missions have failed. Their colonization is not even a name. With such a record in the past, no pressure surely can be required to make the Government of England stand firm in its repudiation of a claim which, were it acknowledged, would destroy the last hope for East Central Africa.

England's stake in this country is immeasurably greater than any statistics can represent, but a rough estimate of the tangible English interest will show

the necessity of the British Government doing its
utmost at least to conserve what is already there.

The Established Church of Scotland has three
ordained missionaries in the Shiré Highlands, one
medical man, a male and a female teacher, a carpenter,
a gardener, and other European and many native
agents. The Free Church of Scotland on Lake
Nyassa has four ordained missionaries—three of whom
are doctors—several teachers and artizans, and many
native catechists. The Universities Mission possesses
a steamer on Lake Nyassa, and several missionary
agents ; while the African Lakes Company, as already
mentioned, has steamers both on the Shiré and Lake
Nyassa, with twelve trading stations established at
intervals throughout the country, and manned by
twenty-five European agents. All these various
agencies, and that of the brothers Buchanan at Zomba,
are well equipped with buildings, implements, roads,
plantations, and gardens ; and the whole represents
a capital expenditure of not less than £180,000.
The well-known editor of Livingstone's Journals, the
Rev. Horace Waller, thus sums up his account of
these English enterprises in his *Title-Deeds to Nyassa-
Land :* "Dotted here and there, from the mangrove
swamps at the Kongoné mouth of the Zambesi to the
farthest extremity of Lake Nyassa, we pass the graves
of naval officers, of brave ladies, of a missionary
bishop, of clergymen, Foreign Office representatives,
doctors, scientific men, engineers, and mechanics.
All these were our countrymen : they lie in glorious
graves ; their careers have been foundation-stones,
and already the edifice rises. British mission stations
are working at high pressure on the Shiré Highlands,
and under various auspices, not only upon the shores
of Lake Nyassa, but on its islands also, and, by
desperate choice as it were, in the towns of the
devastating hordes who live on the plateaux on
either side of the lake. Numbers of native Christians
owe their knowledge of the common faith to these

efforts; scores of future chiefs are being instructed
in the schools, spread over hundreds of miles; plantations are being mapped out; commerce is developing
by sure and steady steps; a vigorous company is
showing to tribes and nations that there are more
valuable commodities in their land than their sons
and daughters." This is the vision which Livingstone saw, when, in the last years of his life, he
pleaded with his fellow-countrymen to follow him
into Africa. "I have opened the door," he said, "I
leave it to you to see that no one closes it after me."

The urgency of the question of Portuguese as
against British supremacy in Equatorial Africa must
not blind us, however, to another and scarcely less
important point—the general European, and especially the recent German, invasion of Africa. The
Germans are good, though impecunious colonists,
but it cannot be said that they or any of the other
European nations are as alive to the moral responsibilities of administration among native tribes as
England would desire. And though they are all
freely entitled to whatever lands in Africa they may
legitimately secure, it is advisable for all concerned
that these acquisitions should be clearly defined and
established in international law, in order that the
various Powers, the various trading-companies, and
the various missions, may know exactly where they
stand. The almost hopeless entanglement of the
Foreign Powers in Africa at present may be seen
from the following political "section," which represents the order of occupation along the Atlantic sea-
board from opposite Gibraltar to the Cape:—

POLITICAL "SECTION" OF WESTERN AFRICA.

Spain	. . .	Morocco.
France	. . .	"
Spain	. . .	Opposite the Canaries.
France	.	French Senegambia.

Britain	.	.	. British Senegambia
France	.	.	. French "
Britain	.	.	. British "
Portugal	.	.	. Portuguese "
France	.	.	
Britain	.	.	. Sierra Leone.
Liberia	.	.	. Republic of Liberia.
France	.	.	. Gold Coast.
England	.	.	. Gold Coast.
France	.	.	. Dahomey.
Unappropriated	.	.	"
England	.	.	. Niger.
Germany	.	.	. Cameroons.
French	.	.	. French Congo.
Portuguese	.	.	. Portuguese Congo.
International	.	.	. Congo.
Portuguese	.	.	. Angola.
Portuguese	.	.	. Benguela.
Germany	.	.	. Angra Pequena.
England	.	.	. Walvisch Bay.
Germany	.	.	. Orange River.
England	.	.	. Cape of Good Hope.

These several possessions on the western coast
have at least the advantage of being to some extent
defined, but those on the east, and especially as
regards their inland limits, are in a complete state
of chaos. It seems hopeless to propose it, but what
is really required is an International Conference to
overhaul title-deeds, adjust boundary-lines, delimit
territories, mark off states, protectorates, lands held
by companies, and spheres of influence. England's
interest in this must be largely a moral one. Her
ambitions in the matter of new territories are long
ago satisfied. But there will be certain conflict some
day if the portioning of Africa is not more closely
watched than it is at present.

As an example of the complacent way in which
vast tracts in Africa are being appropriated, glance
for a moment at the recent inroads of the Germans.
On the faith of private treaties, and of an agreement

with Portugal, Germany has recently staked off a region in East Central Africa stretching from the boundaries of the Congo Free State to the Indian Ocean, and embracing an area considerably larger than the German Empire. To a portion only of this region—the boundaries of which, contrasted with that arbitrarily claimed in addition, will be apparent from a comparison of the maps—have the Germans procured a title; and the steps by which this has been attained afford an admirable illustration of modern methods of land-transfer in Africa. What happened was this:—

Four or five years ago Dr. Karl Peters concluded treaties with the native chiefs of Useguha, Ukami, Nguru and Usagara, by which he acquired these territories from the Society for German Colonization. The late Sultan of Zanzibar attempted to remonstrate, but meantime an imperial "Schutzbrief" had been secured from Berlin, and a German fleet arrived at Zanzibar prepared to enforce it. Britain appealed to Germany on the subject, and a Delimitation Commission was appointed, which met in London. An agreement was come to, signed by Lord Iddesleigh on 29th October, 1886, and duly given effect to. The terms of this Anglo-German Convention have been recently made public in a well-informed article by Mr. A. Silva White (*Scottish Geographical Magazine*, March, 1888), to which I am indebted for some of the above facts, and the abstract may be given here intact, as political knowledge of Africa is not only deficient, but materials for improving it are all but inaccessible. In view, moreover, of the spirit of acquisitiveness which is abroad among the nations of Europe, and of recent attempts on the part of Germany to claim more than her title allows, the exact terms of this contract ought to be widely known :—

I. Both Powers recognize the sovereignty of the Sultan of Zanzibar over the islands of Zanzibar and Pemba, Lamu and Mafia, as also over those small islands lying within a circuit of twelve nautical miles of Zanzibar. Both Powers also recognize as the Sultan's possessions on the mainland an uninterrupted coast-line from the mouth of the Miningani River at the entrance of the bay of Tunghi (south of Cape Delgado) as far as Kipini (south of Wito). This line encloses a coast of ten nautical miles inland for the whole distance. The northern boundary includes Kau ; north of Kipini, both Powers recognize as belonging to the Sultan of Zanzibar the stations of Kisimayu, Brava, Merka, and Makdishu (Magadoxo), each with a land circuit of ten nautical miles, and Warsheikh with a land circuit of five nautical miles.

II. Great Britain engages herself to support those negotiations of Germany with the Sultan which have for their object the farming out (*Verpachtung*) of the customs in the harbors of Dar-es-Salaam and Pangani to the German East African Association, on the payment by the Association to the Sultan of an annual guaranteed sum of money.

III. Both Powers agree to undertake a delimitation of their respective spheres of influence in this portion of the East African Continent. This territory shall be considered as bounded on the south by the Rovuma River, and on the north by a line, commencing from the mouth of the Tana River, following the course of this river or its tributaries, to the intersection of the Equator with the 38th degree of east longitude, and from thence continued in a straight line to the intersection of the 1st degree of north latitude with the 37th degree of east longitude. The line of demarcation shall start from the mouth of the river Wanga, or Umbe, and follow a straight course to Lake Jipé (southeast of Kilima-njaro), along the eastern shore and round the northern shore of the lake, across the river Lumi, passing between the territories of Taveta and Chagga, and then along the northern slope of the Kilima-njaro range and continued in a straight line to the point on the eastern shore of Lake Victoria Nyanza which is intersected by the 1st degree of south latitude.

Great Britain engages herself to make no territorial acquisitions, to accept no Protectorates, and not to compete with the spread of German influence to the south of this line, whilst Germany engages herself to observe a similar abstinence in the territories to the north of this line,

IV. Great Britain will use her influence to promote the conclusion of a friendly agreement concerning the existing claims of the Sultan of Zanzibar and the German East African Association, on the Kilima-njaro territory.

V. Both Powers recognize as belonging to Wito the coast stretching from the north of Kipini to the north end of Manda Bay.

VI. Great Britain and Germany will conjointly call upon the Sultan of Zanzibar to recognize the General Act of the Berlin Conference, save and except the existing rights of His Highness as laid down in Art. I. of the Act.

VII. Germany binds herself to become a party to the Note signed by Great Britain and France on 10th March, 1862, in regard to the recognition of the independence of Zanzibar.

This is the only document which can have any validity, and such German claims—outside the limit here assigned—as are represented on the newer German maps, are to be treated as mere chartographical flourishes. Encouraged, however, by this success in securing territory in Africa, and without stopping to use or even to proclaim their protectorate over more than a fraction of the petty states comprised within it, the Germans instantly despatched expedition after expedition to secure further conquest in the remoter and unappropriated districts. Dr. Karl Peters himself led one large expedition; Dr. Jühlke negotiated agreements with the tribes on the distant Somal coast; and other explorers brought back rare and heavy spoil—on paper—to Berlin. So the swallowing up of Africa goes on. The slices cut are daily becoming bigger, and in a few years more not a crumb of the loaf will remain for those who own it now. The poor Sultan of Zanzibar, who used to boast himself lord of the whole interior, woke up, after the London Convention, to find that his African kingdom consisted of a ten-mile-wide strip of coast-line, extending from Kipini to the Miningani River. Even this has already been sold or leased to the English and Germans, and nothing now remains to His Highness but a few small islands.

Since turning her attention towards Africa, Germany has not only looked well after new territory, but seized the opportunity to inspect and readjust the title-deeds to her other African property. We find a new treaty concluded in 1885 between her and the British Protectorate in the Niger regarding the Cameroons; another towards the close of the same year with France on the same subject, and securing rights to Malimba and Great Batonga; and a third with Portugal in 1887, defining, in the interest of the latter, the boundaries of Angola, and ceding to Germany, as a *quid-pro-quo,* an acknowledgment of the claim of the Germans—which, of course, England repudiates—to East Central Africa from the coast to the south end of Tanganyika and Lake Nyassa, as far as the latitude of the Rovuma.

These facts prove the genuine political activity of at least one great European power, and offer a precedent to England, which, in one respect at least, she would do well to copy. Her title-deeds, and those of certain districts in which she is concerned, are not in such perfect order as to justify the apathy which exists at present, and her interests in the country are now too serious to be the prey of unchallenged ambitions, or left at the mercy of any casual turn of the wheel of politics.

Thanks, partly, to the recent seizure by Portugal of the little Zambesi steamer belonging to the African Lakes company—on the plea that vessels trading on Portuguese waters must be owned by Portuguese subjects, and fly the Portuguese flag—and to influential deputations to head-quarters on the part of the various Missions, the Foreign Office is beginning to be alive to the state of affairs in East Central Africa. The annexation of Matabeleland will be a chief item on the programme with which it is hoped the Government will shortly surprise us; but, what is of greater significance, it will probably include a declaration of the Zambesi as an open river, and the abolition or serious restriction of the present customs tariff. Important as these things are, however, they affect but slightly the two supreme English interests in East Central Africa—the suppression of the slave-trade and the various missionary and industrial enterprises. The most eager among the supporters of these higher interests have never ventured to press upon Government anything so pronounced as that England should declare a Protectorate over the Upper Shiré and Nyassa districts; but they do contend, and with every reason, for the delimitation of part of this region as a "Sphere of British Influence."

Granting even that the shadowy claims of Germany and Portugal to the eastern shore of Lake Nyassa are to be respected, there remain the whole western coast of the Lake, and the regions of the Upper Shiré which are reached directly from the waters of the Zambesi without trespassing on the soil of any nation. These regions are not even claimed at present by any one, while by every right of discovery and occupation—by every right, in fact, except that of formal acknowledgment—they are already British. It will be an oversight most culpable and inexcusable if this great theatre of British missionary and trading activity should be allowed to be picked up by any passing traveller, or become the property of whatever European power had sufficient effrontery at this late day to wave its flag over it. The thriving settlements, the schools and churches, the roads and trading-stations, of Western Nyassa-land are English. And yet it is neither asked that they should be claimed by England, annexed by England, nor protected by England. Those whose inspirations and whose lives have created this oasis in the desert, plead only that no intruder now should be allowed to undo their labor or idly reap its fruits. Here is one spot, at least, on the Dark Continent, which is being kept pure and clean. It is now within the power of the

English Government to mark it off before the world
as henceforth sacred ground.   To-morrow, it may be
too late.

————

X.

A METEOROLOGICAL NOTE.

The Lake Nyassa region of Africa knows only
two seasons—the rainy and the dry.   The former
begins with great regularity on the opening days of
December, and closes towards the end of April ; while
during the dry season, which follows for the next
six months, the sun is almost never darkened with a
cloud.   At Blantyre, on the Shiré Highlands, the
rainfall averages fifty inches ; at Bandawé, on Lake
Nyassa, a register of eighty-six inches is counted a
somewhat dryish season.

The barometer in tropical countries is much more
conservative of change than in northern latitudes,
and the annual variation at Lake Nyassa is only
about half an inch——or from 28·20 inches in November to 28·70 inches in June.   The diurnal variation,
according to Mr. Stewart, is rarely more than twenty-
hundredths of an inch.

The average temperature for the year at Blantyre,
where the elevation is about three thousand feet
above sea-level, is 50° Fahr., but the mercury has
been known to stand ten degrees lower, and on one
exceptional occasion it fell 2° below freezing point.
At Lake Nyassa, half the height of Blantyre, 85°
Fahr. is a common figure for mid-day in the hottest
month (November) in the year, while the average
night-temperature of the coldest month (May) is
about 60°.   The lowest registered temperature on
the Lake has been 54°, and the highest—though this
is extremely rare—100° Fahr.   When the Livingstonia Mission occupied the promontory of Cape

Maclear, at the southern end of Nyassa, in 1880, one of the then staff, Mr. Harkess, had the energy to keep a systematic record of the temperature, and I am indebted to his notebook for the following table. The figures represent observations taken at 6 A.M., 12 noon, and 6 P.M. A dash indicates that the observation was omitted for the hour corresponding. The wet bulb reads on an average 10 degrees lower.

TABLE OF TEMPERATURES AT LAKE NYASSA.

	May	June	July	Aug.	Sept.		May	June	July	Aug.	Sept.
1	70	62	64	67	68	10	67	68	66	61	—
	80	75	73	74	79		75	75	—	81	80
	75	76	74	73	75		74	73	71	—	77
2	—	60	64	68	69	11	69	66	—	62	70
	77	78	74	—	79		75	76	76	79	79
	—	73	—	74	75		—	75	73	—	79
3	67	65	62	65	66	12	—	66	69	65	—
	76	78	74	—	75		75	75	77	81	—
	76	74	70	—	74		71	72	—	76	—
4	68½	64	—	62	71	13	65	—		70	72
	79	71	73	—	77		76	73		80	79
	78	70	—	—	79		74	—		77	78
5	68	64	63	76	—	14	67	63		68	71
	79	74	—	—	—		73	74		77	81
	76	74	71	—	—		71	—		75	78
6	—	64	64	70	65	15	68	64	—	66	72
	75½	77	72	77	81		76	74	—	—	75
	75	76	74	—	77		75	72	76	—	77
7	66	67	64	61	72	16	71	64	68	67	—
	79	78	71	79	80		77	74	79	75	79
	75	75	71	—	77		75	70	78	73	77
8	65	66	64	—	70	17	68	64	65	—	—
	74	74	—	—	80		78	74	77	—	—
	74	74	71	—	81		77	72	—	76	76
9	—	68	65	62	70	18	72	71	68	68	73
	77	76	75	79	81		80	74	75	75	78
	—	73	73	—	77		78	72	76	72	77

	May	June	July	Aug.	Sept.		May	June	July	Aug.	Sept.
19	65	64	69	--	—	26	67	63	67	64	—
	74	—	77	75	—		75	75	79	72	—
	76	77	79	74	—		75	—	76	73	—
20	63	—	67	68	75	27	69	—	65	65	73
	74	76	76	—	82		77	72	74	77	84
	76	74	74	75	80		74	—	71	77	82
21	67	65	64	64	71	28	70	—	65	70	73
	75	72	75	—	85		78	72	76	79	81
	75	68	75	75	78		77	—	74	78	79
22	70	63	67	—	72	29	68	63	65	—	68
	75	66	75	78	81		80	71	72	76	82
	—	65	76	75	79		77	72	75	—	80
23		58	65	—	70	30	—	64	63	67	74
		67	77	79	82		75	74	78	79	82
		70	74	77	78		76	—	75	77	80
24	—	62	64	68	73	31	67		65	66	
	76	—	76	69	82		74		76	79	
	76	—	74	66	81		74		76	83	
25	67	61	66	63	74						
	77	—	74	75	—						
	75	—	75	71	78